D1109602

GARIBALDI

THE STRATFORD LIBRARY

GARIBALDI

DENIS MACK SMITH

HUTCHINSON OF LONDON

HUTCHINSON & CO (*Publishers*) **LTD**
178–202 Great Portland Street, London, W.1

London Melbourne Sydney
Auckland Bombay Toronto
Johannesburg New York

First published 1957

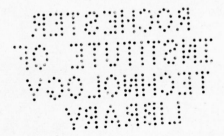

ROCHESTER
INSTITUTE OF
TECHNOLOGY
LIBRARY

*Set in ten point Linotype Caledonia one point leaded
and printed in Great Britain by
Taylor Garnett Evans & Co. Ltd
Watford, Hertfordshire*

CONTENTS

55147

551 47

GARIBALDI

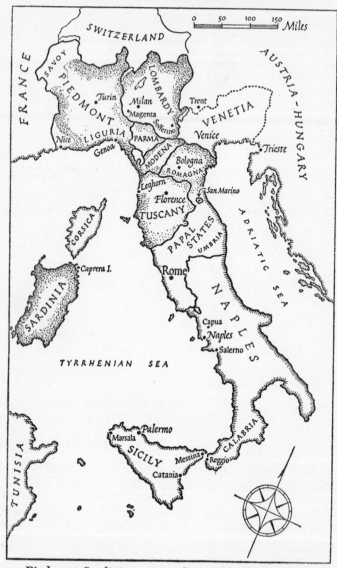

Piedmont-Sardinia acquired Lombardy in 1859, the centre in March 1860, Umbria and the south in November 1860, Venetia in 1866, and Rome in 1870

CHAPTER ONE

APPRENTICESHIP

1807-1834

WITH all his failings, Giuseppe Garibaldi is firmly fixed among the great men of the nineteenth century. He was great first of all as a national hero, a soldier and sailor of renown to whom more than anyone else was due the union of northern and southern Italy. But as well as a nationalist he was also a great internationalist, and with him this was no paradox. He was a professional liberator, a man who fought for oppressed people wherever he found them. Although essentially a fighter and man of action, at the same time he managed to be an idealist sharply marked out from his more hardheaded contemporaries. Whatever he did was done with passionate conviction and boundless enthusiasm, and a career full of colour and incident makes him now seem one of the most romantic products of his age. Besides, he was a lovable and fascinating person of transparent honesty whom men would obey unhesitatingly and for whom they were glad to die. Ordinary people felt him to be one of themselves, for he was the very embodiment of the common man. Yet he was also someone quite exceptional, a real individual and nonconformist whether in his religion, his clothes, his personal habits, or the events of his extraordinary life.

Garibaldi's tracks are not always easy to follow, partly because of these very idiosyncrasies of belief and behaviour. Many legends grew up about his name, and many inventions were consciously or unconsciously grafted on to the record by his friends and adorers. Even his autobiography appeared in a number of different versions after its first publication in New York in English. For though he was a forthright person who lacked ulterior motives, his memory was poor, and he often rewrote his memoirs, sometimes employing the aid of professional writers such as Dumas who liked a good story as much as they liked the truth.

Again, his career is not documented as would be the life of a prominent statesman. There were no close disciples to annotate his every movement and thought, and his own letters were those of an extrovert who obstinately spoke of things other than himself. Until he was over fifty there were few people who took him seriously. His guerrilla armies melted away and left no archives, nor were his battles fought on any elaborate and prearranged plan that can be precisely re-created. Garibaldi, though he always imposed his own tremendous spirit on his soldiers, liked to fight on the spur of the moment and as the moment directed. He worked by instinct and intuition, and his tactical successes and failures were mostly impromptu combinations that dissolve under the purview of scientific history.

And yet, though the details may be questionable and sometimes lacking altogether, the impression that remains is clear-cut, for he was such a colossal character that the whole has more verisimilitude than the parts. A genuine simplicity and integrity make him a personality in the round, picturesque and admirable, while his association with great events makes him someone of no little historical importance.

The life of Giuseppe Garibaldi stretched between the years 1807 and 1882. Not much is known about his childhood, and it contained, so he said himself, nothing extraordinary. Nevertheless, the chief events in the early years of a man always hold a certain interest in the light of his later achievements, and, without being oversubtle, one can usually trace there something of those governing influences which help to fuse the complex amalgam of a human personality.

He was born on the edge of the Alps in Nice, which at that time was part of Napoleonic France. Not until he was seven did Nice join up again with an independent Piedmont under the dynasty of Savoy. The language he grew up to speak was the local Ligurian dialect, and the second tongue of the neighbourhood was French. Later on he set himself to speak Italian, but his accent, grammar, and spelling always betrayed that it came not quite naturally. This whole setting may help just a little to explain the frontier-consciousness and exaggerated nationalism of his middle years. His fair hair and light-coloured eyes—they were brown, but many admirers deceived themselves to think that they were blue—betokened a northern origin and contributed to make him an object of veneration to the dark-haired, dark-skinned southerners from Naples and Sicily.

Nice was on the sea, and Garibaldi's father was a sailor and the son of a sailor. The sea was in their blood. They were traders and fisherfolk, humble but not poor. Although they had a very strong family feeling, like all Ligurians they were accustomed by the poverty of this coast land to seek their fortune overseas, and an elder brother, Angelo, made good abroad and ended up as a consul in Philadelphia. Their mother was a sweet character, and for her Garibaldi came to have a sort of cult. She overwhelmed him with a tenderness that he himself called almost excessive, and it was her picture, not that of any of his three wives, which remained always above his bed.

No one would ever have accused Garibaldi of being an intellectual, but neither was he the uneducated boor that his enemies called him. His parents had hoped that he might become a lawyer or even a priest, and their misplaced efforts left him with the latent grumble that Italian education was geared to the manufacture of lawyers and priests rather than of good citizens and soldiers. It cannot have been easy to teach someone of his truant disposition, yet he carried into later life enough mathematics, astronomy, and geography to become an expert navigator, and enough history and literature to chance his hand as a schoolmaster on two occasions when out of a job. His friends thought they could remember that as a boy he would read abstractedly for hours under the olive trees, and in later years his few shelves of books contained mostly the classics of world literature. He had learned all the songs of the peasants and sailors, and retained a fondness for singing folk songs and for the recitation of stirring poetry.

Until he was over forty the sea was his element. In earliest youth he used to run off trawling for oysters and sardines. He never remembered learning to swim, but seemed to have been born amphibious, and a dozen or more times it was to be recorded that he saved people from drowning. The first occasion was when only eight years old, and this early incident seems almost to have cast him for a lifetime in the rôle of a hero. His actions and daydreams show that he developed a conscious fixation and urge to be heroic, to deliver all victims of misfortune and oppression and make the world a freer and healthier place. It was not an unworthy or unnatural instinct; only the times seemed unpropitious.

At first Garibaldi's parents were afraid to let him go to sea. He and some other boys once ran off in a fishing-smack towards Genoa and had to be overtaken and brought home. So restive and ungovernable was he that finally he won his point, and when only fifteen travelled all the way to Odessa as a cabin boy. This was in a 225-ton brigantine sailing under the Russian flag to fetch a cargo of grain from the Black Sea.

Another journey took place in 1825, when he set out with his father in a small thirty-tonner to Rome, being drawn by oxen up the Tiber with a load of wine. Over a month they stayed in the holy city, and the visit must have left a deep impression. His pious father was on pilgrimage for the Holy Year, but Garibaldi's most vivid memory was of pre-Christian Rome, a reminder of when the city had been imperial mistress of the known world. Ancient history was to become a passion with him; so was a conviction that the desolate Papal Rome of 1825 must be delivered from clerical rule and become the capital of a new Italian nation. His private rebellion against priestly education was thus to be projected on to a wider plane.

Between 1825 and 1832 Garibaldi was almost always cruising to and from the eastern Mediterranean and the Black Sea. Once, when at Constantinople, he fell ill and was left behind, and for some months had to earn his living at tutor to a private family. Three times in these dangerous eastern waters he was assaulted and despoiled by pirates, and on one occasion was wounded. This was his first training in war. Here he developed his toughness, his love of risk and adventure, and his liking for solitude and travel. These voyages gave him a precise instruction in seamanship, and enabled him in 1832 to take his master's certificate as a trained sea captain. They taught him self-reliance and freedom from all governments. They helped to shape his cosmopolitan turn of mind and secure him friends in many lands. They also allowed him to see how the Greeks and others were achieving national independence against the effete empires of Turkey and Austria, and this suggested that his own country might be falling behind the times.

Garibaldi was a man capable of strong feeling and easily enslaved by any generous and humane idea. Quite early he was captivated by a watered-down version of Saint-Simon doctrine of universal brotherhood and the extinction of classes. But of all the dominating forces in his life, the idea of freedom and unification for Italy was to be the strongest. It was probably on a journey to Taganrog in 1833 that he first met and was fascinated by some of the early disciples of this new and revolutionary creed.

Italy was at that time divided into some eight different states all of them under more or less reactionary and unenlightened governments. Austria was a pervasive and dominant influence throughout the peninsula, but even the native Italian dynasties were stubbornly set against the new doctrines of liberalism and nationalism. Only a handful of Italians were so discontented and visionary as to talk of a national revolution and the formation of a united Italian republic. These revolutionaries were led by Giuseppe Mazzini, and he had lately formed a secret society called "Young Italy" to propagate his views. Late in 1833, in the suburbs of Marseilles, Garibaldi was taken to see the exiled Mazzini and enrolled in the society. Here he took an oath in the name of God and the martyrs of Italy to fight against injustice, oppression, and tyranny, and to make an Italian nation one and free. Thus he was "initiated into the sublime mysteries of the fatherland": it was to be the first step in a lifetime of revolution, and he determined to do what he could to further the cause in his own state of Piedmont.

Just because he now became a conspirator, this is an obscure period in Garibaldi's history, especially as he went about under three or four assumed names. He was not yet a great man whose doings were news-worthy. His later differences with Mazzini led him in retrospect to colour what had happened, and so to antedate his conversion to nationalism and conceal the fact that he had been to see the great revolutionary. He also described in later days how he volunteered to join the Piedmontese navy as a first-class sailor in order to help engineer a nationalist insurrection that was planned to break out at Genoa in 1834. In fact, he seems to have been called up in December 1833 for service with the navy as a conscript sailor third class, and for a few weeks wore the black tailcoat and top hat of the official uniform.

A feeble attempt at insurrection duly took place early in 1834, but served only to show that neither Garibaldi nor his new friends had the first idea about how to organize a successful conspiracy. He himself was lucky enough to escape into the mountains, dis-guised as a peasant by a woman who sold fruit in Genoa. Ten days he spent walking by unfreqented paths to Nice, and there greatly shocked his God-fearing, law-abiding parents with the story of what had happened. Then he fled over the frontier to France, was arrested and escaped, and avoided a second arrest by showing that he could sing French popular songs. At Genoa, meanwhile, in his absence he had been condemned to death for high treason by the very government of Piedmont which in later years he was to serve so well.

So ended, not very heroically, Garibaldi's first venture in revolutionary politics. At the age of twenty-six he was an outlaw, and he had to remain in exile for the next thirteen years. Apart from this, there was nothing very remarkable about him, and it does not seem that he possessed the imposing, fascinating personality of later days. He was a rough, honest sailor, good enough at his job, enterprising and adventurous but prejudicing his career by naïve political enthusiasms.

The naval recruiting records show him as a shortish man of five and a half feet, or a little more. He had reddish hair, and liked to wear it flowing over his shoulders. People noted a feminine delicacy about him, a liking for frequent baths and minute attention to hands, teeth and hair, and all of this must be fitted in with the manly legend of his subsequent life as a husky soldier. He was slightly bow-legged, and indeed it was only his face that was really impressive. The word *beauty* was often used of him, for he had a fine forehead and the profile of a Greek statue. His eyes were sparkling and fascinating, and his smile was soon to make sensible people lose their faculties of judgement. Above all, an open-air boyhood had left him with a nervous energy and wiry constitution that could survive enormous hardship and strain. It was not long before he would need all the strength, all the courage and fascination he could command.

CHAPTER TWO

THE RIO GRANDE

1835-1840

GARIBALDI'S first months of exile were spent in Marseilles, living on the bounty of a friend, with every now and then some odd job on a trading-vessel. For a short while he was even driven to take service with Hussein, the Bey of Tunis, who was trying to reform his navy along European lines. This was a strange uniform for Garibaldi the liberator, and after a month or two he signed on with a Turkish ship and returned to France. Back at Marseilles, he volunteered to help for a few days in a hospital during an outbreak of cholera. It was still an unsatisfactory existence, cheerless and unrewarding, and in 1835 he made a big decision and fled from it on a French ship to Brazil. Many Italians were now accustomed to regard South America as the promised land. The great migration had begun that was to reach nearly a million a year at its peak, and already whole villages along the Genoese coastline were depopulated by people running away from unemployment to seek their fortune in the New World. Garibaldi was thus one of many.

Not until 1848 did he come back to Europe, and by that time half of his adult life had been spent in South America. This period had the greatest formative influence on his character. Here he learned to live hard, free as the air, a law unto himself in a land where nature was cruel and life was cheap. It was a world of piracy and banditry where refugees from all the nations of Europe jostled in an atmosphere of fierce cut-throat rivalries and primitive superstition. Fighting was a normal occupation, and a man depended on his own right arm because the hand of every man was against his neighbour. Everyone appeared to display a passionate love of freedom, but it was an anarchical sort of freedom which blurred easily into factionalism and ruthless dictatorship.

Between the ages of twenty-eight and forty Garibaldi thus lived for the most part as a corsair and soldier of adventure in selfish faction fights that he, in his innocent unselfishness, thought to be the cause of freedom pure and unadulterated. It was a good school of war, but hardly of politics. He learned to think of the pampas rancher as an ideal type of person, and for the rest of his life always tended to dress and behave as a *caudillo* at the head of his Gauchos. When finally he returned to Italy as a national leader, these Spanish-American customs were often a factor in both his triumphs and failures. Italian history was going to be very different as a result.

In Rio de Janeiro, Garibaldi was not immediately involved in local politics, for his mind still centred on Europe. He joined the local branch of "Young Italy" and preached the doctrine that all peoples of the world should unite to fight oppression and regenerate the human race. In January 1836, only a few days after arrival, he wrote to Mazzini that he hoped the war for Italian liberation would start within the year, and he asked for letters of marque empowering him to wage private war on the shipping of Piedmont and Austria. The Piedmontese minister reported that the revolutionary tricolour flag was flown over the house where these Italian radicals met. Some of the Piedmontese ships in the harbour, the minister added, had agreed to watch their chance and stealthily sink any boats belonging to the revolutionaries, as this was something that could be done at Rio with impunity.

One Italian had given Garibaldi enough money to buy a small fishing-boat, and he began to trade up and down the coast with flour, sugar and brandy. But it was a poor business. While other Italians were making their fortunes, he was not nearly sharp enough for commerce. He was too artless, too trustful of human nature—and probably also too bored—to make a respectable living. He still had not found his *métier*.

The Brazilian empire was too large an area to be easily governed as one state, and its southernmost province, the Rio Grande do Sul, was trying to assert its independence. The first president of this breakaway state was Benito Gonçalves, whose secretary was an Italian friend of Garibaldi's. The cause of liberty was not very obviously involved in this fruitless provincial war of liberation, and Garibaldi later acknowledged that he had never had much quarrel with Brazil; but he was not yet the man to see farther than immediate sympathies and loyalties, and instinctively he recognized the kind of life he wanted to lead. It was enough that his friend was involved and that the word *liberty* was on all tongues.

Moreover, Gonçalves was a brave and magnanimous warrior—perhaps ill-fated and unsuccessful, but in all other respects a perfect model to admire and copy. The president was indeed a copybook romantic leader and popular hero: a person of humble tastes who usually managed to play the friendly, courteous cavalier, a fine horseman, picturesque in dress, enthusiastically followed by his men—it is a perfect picture of Garibaldi twenty years later, and the resemblance is probably not altogether accidental.

In May 1837 a boat of about twenty tons, signifi-

cantly called the *Mazzini,* started out from the Rio
Grande with a crew of half a dozen to prey on
Brazilian shipping. This might have seemed like the
instinctive reaction of Italians in hard times to take to
the life of a pirate or partisan against oppressive
government. Some of Garibaldi's friends, who personally had more ability in trade and more sense than to
adopt a brigand's life, helped to fit out his expedition.
For three years he was to fight against Brazil, and then
for the best part of six more years against Argentina.
At last he was happy and master of his own fate. "The
ocean was mine," he wrote, "and I took possession of
my element."

It was a Robin-Hood life fighting for the underdog,
an existence that offered plenty of scope for courage,
enterprise, and chivalry, and provided the warm but
unexamined conviction that he was on the side of
justice and freedom. Garibaldi may not have been too
scrupulous about which ships he attacked, but at least
his main object was not booty; never in his life did
money mean anything to him. On occasion he could
be as ambitious and warlike and rancorous as any other
caudillo, but it was not in his nature to be ungenerous
or cruel; he was never hardheaded or out for personal
gain. Indeed, he was too much of a romantic and an
idealist ever to be a mere soldier of fortune. His
ambition was never vulgar ambition.

This was Byron's corsair in action. It was a perilous
life, though full of romance. Their first capture was an
Austrian brig carrying a Brazilian cargo of coffee; and
in his later recollections Garibaldi proudly claimed
that five Negro slaves were freed, and also that he
refused to take some diamonds from a Portuguese. In
June 1837 he was painfully wounded during the first
serious fight of his life. His companion having been
killed, he seized the tiller, only to be himself "mortally

wounded" (he said) by a ball that entered his neck under one ear and buried itself under the other. It was ten days before he could reach a doctor ashore, but his physique was like iron and his heart invincible.

Not long afterwards he was taken prisoner. Finding an excuse to break his parole, he escaped, but then, recaptured, he was whipped and strung up by his arms and carried for miles on horseback with hands and feet tied while the mosquitoes stung his flesh "into a single wound". Even if these tales were coloured in retrospect, it must have been an existence that only the fittest would survive, and the crippling arthritis and rheumatism of his later years may well have been due in part to this strained and exhausting way of life.

Garibaldi used to recollect the Rio Grande as one of the most beautiful parts of the world, and his leisure life on some *estancia* remained among his happiest memories. "The wilder the country, the more beautiful I thought it," even the almost impassable swamps and jungle where he sometimes had to flee for his life through torrents of rain and eat nothing but roots. In normal times when ashore he and his men lived off meat roasted in the open at every meal. This suited his open-air disposition, though perhaps it helped turn him to vegetarianism in later years. Their enemies were ten times stronger and better supplied, but to such a man this gave the life an added zest and savour. He loved the constant movement and activity, in the companionship of brave men who lived simply and fought for what they thought was right. With them, he wrote, "I first learned how to despise danger and to fight for the sacred cause of nationality".

In 1838-1839 the Rio Grande fleet consisted of two launches, the second commanded by a United States citizen, John Griggs. All told, their complement was about seventy men, many of them Negro slaves escaped from the north, but including seven Italians. This cosmopolitan crew "I treated with perhaps excessive kindness, not then knowing much about human nature". For the first time Garibaldi discovered how effortlessly he could win obedience by the natural reverence and affection that his personality commanded from all and sundry.

The Brazilians were able to use thirty ships to blockade this tiny force, and once the two launches had to escape overland, dragged by a hundred pairs of oxen. In July 1839 one of them was lost in a squall, as it was too heavily laden. Garibaldi at the time was up the mast looking for an emergency harbour and so was thrown free; but only fourteen men survived, and among these were none of the Italians, not a single one of his intimate friends. This came as a tremendous shock, and in his loneliness he determined to look about him for a wife.

He thus described his state of mind:

"I had never considered matrimony, and indeed thought myself incapable of it because of my over-independent nature and my bent towards an adventurous career. To have a wife and children seemed to be altogether unseemly in one who had consecrated his entire life to a principle! ... But now, lonely and friendless, pacing the quarterdeck of my ship, I turned the whole question over in my mind, and finally decided to search out a woman of my heart."

This was why he carefully scanned the shore through his telescope; and one day in this strange manner he suddenly made his choice. Going straightway ashore, by his own account, he sought out the lady he had scrutinized and simply told her: "You must be mine." This was a cool insolence that seems to fit the character and the place. Only once did he ever refer publicly to what happened, and then he told only part of the truth. What he never confessed was that Anita was married and had been for some years, and that he carried her off after accepting her husband's hospitality. His silence, and certain other guarded statements, seem to show that in later years he reproached himself for taking her away in this manner to a tragic death in Italy.

Anna Ribeiro da Silva was a dark-skinned beauty. An English naval officer remembered her as a creole with real Spanish dignity. She must have been of mixed Indian and Portuguese descent. These rebel ships off the shore would have been a novelty in her monotonous life, and as Garibaldi was already a local hero, we may assume that it was a not unwilling elope- ment when in October 1839 she embarked to help fight the Brazilian imperialists. Many are the stories of her courage, her endurance, and her fierce jealousy. Like other women in her position, she followed her husband to the wars and took part in many fights, even being captured and having to escape under all manner of privations. Their eldest son, Menotti, was born a year later, and in 1842 they were married.

Anita's home was the neighbouring province of Santa Catarina, whose unsolicited "liberation" by the republicans of Rio Grande had been a little too forcible. The inhabitants of Santa Catarina were soon them- selves in rebellion against the violent and despotic rule of these self-styled liberators, and manifestly preferred the loose rein of distant albeit "reactionary" Brazil. At this, the republicans threw all their affecta- tion of liberalism aside, and Garibaldi was ordered to put one of the rebel cities to the sack in a bestial scene that haunted him for the rest of his life. Such was the hard school of war he was learning in. He was scandalized at how his men got out of hand—drunk, avid for loot, an easy prey to counter-attack by the enemy.

If Garibaldi one day became a great general, it was largely because of the value he learned to place on morale, and on this occasion he received a useful and terrible lesson. In this particular war neither the local inhabitants nor even the soldiers could now see much that was worth fighting about. Desertions were increasing rapidly, especially whenever any immediate danger receded. Civil war is a dreadful thing at best, and this was nowhere near the best. The cause of freedom often was all too obviously a mask for base interests and rival factions competing for the conquest of power. Even the ingenuous Garibaldi became disillusioned as he observed treachery and personal rivalries where he had thought to find a noble and generous cause.

A succession of victories by the Brazilians in 1839-1840 finally decided him to leave the service of the Rio Grande. He described the last bloody scenes of battle, with Anita herself firing the cannon amid mutilated limbs and bodies flying through the air with clothes ablaze. Garibaldi as a commander was never at his best in defeat. He had thought that he was fighting for the people against tyranny and misrule, but now found that the people were not on his side, nor was the tyranny and misgovernment only with his opponents. Never knowingly would he have served a tyrant, but his ideas about tyranny were just too simple to be true. He had hoped that this was a national war, as Mazzini would have wished; but nationality was elusive on the pampas, and it was turning out to be a civil war in which even the Italians were in either camp. No longer was it so easy to think of himself as a knight errant with the intoxicating sensation of being

on the side of the future. Though he was a sentimenta-
list, a romantic, a Quixote, and so could deceive
himself for most of the time, in the long run he, like
everyone else, was vulnerable to the sharp reality of
hard fact.

CHAPTER THREE

MONTEVIDEO

1841-1847

F O R a short time in 1841 Garibaldi settled down once
more to an ordinary peace-time existence. Brazil was
closed to him, so he and his family left on the long
trek down to Montevideo. After the custom of the
country, they drove with them nearly a thousand head
of cattle, intending that the hides and meat should
pay for expenses and set them up in some sort of
business. For fifty days they travelled, but Garibaldi's
ignorance about cattle-droving exposed his unsus-
picious nature to the deceits of his hired men, and
very few of the animals ever arrived at the other end.

At Montevideo he tried his hand as a commercial
traveller in food and textiles. He also taught mathematics and history in a school, and seems to have given
satisfaction. Seven years altogether his family was to
live there, and three more children were born to Anita.
But a civilian life suited him personally not at all, and
most of these seven years he spent fighting for Uruguay
against General Rosas, the tyrant who governed in
the neighbouring Argentine. The courage of a small
people who appeared to be resisting aggression and

tyranny roused him to poetic enthusiasm, and he never could resist the call of hardship and glory.

Once again it is hard to see quite what was at issue in this particular war. But Garibaldi did not investigate the situation too closely, and soon managed to believe that he was fighting for humanity and liberty in general. His own statements at the time abound in references to the cause of humanity and civilization which he thought was at stake.

The republic of Uruguay had not long since declared its independence of Argentina, but was already torn by civil war. The first president, Rivera, had been succeeded in the normal course of events by President Oribe, who had then been deposed by Rivera. Of course Rivera made the usual claim that he was acting on behalf of liberty and the constitution; and perhaps it is true that most urban liberals at first supported him while the landowners were mostly for his rival. But in substance it was just another faction fight, the *blancos* against the *colorados,* with General Rosas of Argentina fishing in troubled waters. This is where we meet Colonel José Garibaldi, as he now signed his name. Looking around for another giant to pit himself against, he enlisted for Rivera against the forces of Oribe and Rosas.

In charge of three ships and three hundred men, he was first assigned the task of forcing his way up the River Paraná in the summer of 1842. It was an absurdly hazardous undertaking with such small resources. His tiny fleet had to penetrate past a much stronger naval squadron and shore batteries and then proceed for some five hundred miles into hostile country, sometimes sailing under a false flag, sometimes running aground in strange waters, trying to destroy enemy commerce as it went, and always risking an encounter with the ships of the Irishman Admiral Brown, who led the defence. Accusations of sack and atrocities were made freely by each side against the other, and probably we ought to modify Garibaldi's self-righteous account of events and assume that barbarities were committed on either side. In August 1842 the expedition was trapped by superior enemy forces in a position from which it could not escape. Part of his force deserted under cover of darkness, and so left the rest at a still greater disadvantage. After a stout resistance he had to burn his boats and escape to shore with such of his men as remained.

Only a few months later the main army of General Rivera was destroyed by Oribe. Private ambitions and rivalries in the government were again a contributory cause of this defeat, and Garibaldi had one more lesson here, if only he could have learned from it, that this sort of war rarely settled anything worth settling. Certainly he began now to develop a lifelong distrust of politicians. He still retained the simple faith that enabled him to pitch headlong into any cause where he thought that justice and right were involved, but increasingly he tried to insist on running his own show without interference from civilians and governments.

The war was taken up again in 1843-1844, but Garibaldi's recollections were imprecise and the chronology is difficult to ascertain. Emergency measures were needed to defend Montevideo. Slaves were liberated to make more soldiers, and strangers in the city were banded together to form foreign legions. The Italian Legion became the pride and joy of Garibaldi. It was only a few hundred strong, and many of its members could come on duty only in the evening after their ordinary work was done. But they constituted something new—almost, as it were, a nucleus of Italian patriotism—and they gave Garibaldi more experience in practical leadership and especially in the problems of organization and discipline. His conduct of discipline, was at this time criticized by some of his men, and he knew himself to be a bad organizer. He needed to become altogether more shrewd and guileful, and at last he began to learn that even the cause of liberty and humanity might need the aid of what he himself now called Machiavellian politics.

It was at this time that Garibaldi developed those fundamental principles of the type of guerrilla warfare which he later made so much his own. Although he did not despise the academic study of tactics—for instance, he made a close study of Nelson's battles, and drew conclusions from them which he then recommended for practical application—he was himself essentially an improviser. Courage and the ability to make quick tactical decisions he thought to be the chief qualities for a fighter. The best general, he used to say, is the general who wins, no matter what military science he possesses. With untrained volunteer troops, a general must pay particular attention to morale. He must fix in his men the unquestioned assumption that he will always win. Cowards who run away should be shot out of hand in order to stop the panic to which raw troops are prone; for human lives are to be considered as nothing in the service of a noble cause. He must always surprise, and never be surprised. He must make a habit of night marches, so as to conceal his numbers from the enemy and avoid the heat of the day. Later in life Garibaldi committed to paper these and other of his favourite military formulas, and they show clear signs of their South American provenance.

In 1843 he was still commanding the Uruguayan fleet, and it was the excitement of leading his own countrymen which made him also take on a land command with the Italian Legion. There were collisions and jealousies at first. Some of the officers even conspired in an attempt to turn him out of his post, and Colonel Mancini then led one group in deserting to the enemy. In fighting qualities, too, it took time before these inexperienced and sometimes slightly disreputable men could be trained and inured to the difficulties of a hard and strenuous life. At their first encounter with the enemy they broke ranks almost without a shot.

Garibaldi had other problems than these. He had to combat the diplomatic action of the Piedmontese consul, who resented such a manifestation of *italianitá* and tried to have the Legion dissolved. Nor was the government always fully behind him, and for a short time he was under arrest for high-handed action against certain private citizens. But in the end this tiny band distinguished itself for great valour and enterprise, and he above all; while more than one future general of the Italian army learned the rudiments of warfare among these amateurs of the art.

The famous red shirts now made their first appearance, chosen perhaps because red was the colour of revolution, but more likely because a consignment of clothes was intercepted on its way for use in the cattle slaughterhouses of Buenos Aires. One of Garibaldi's many picturesque traits was that he liked highly coloured clothes. From this period on, there are to be found innumerable portraits of him, sometimes in naval or army uniform, but usually in the red tunic and Gaucho costume that later became the symbol of Italian nationalism.

Even more picturesque in their way were the small touches of gallantry and chivalry which occasionally took the edge off a sordid civil war. Garibaldi liked the *beau geste,* and could appreciate it in others. He noted with pleasure the magnanimity of Admiral Brown when some unfortunate Montevidean sailors were rescued at sea and put ashore with great courtesies. On another occasion Garibaldi's ships were dramatically saved from Brown when a small skiff flying the British flag moved in time between the opposing forces. Garibaldi himself once planned a reckless commando raid to land by night near Buenos Aires and capture Rosas in his own home, but nothing came of it. Equally typical of him in a quite different vein was the flamboyant gesture with which he publicly turned down several generous gifts made to him and his Legion by Rivera. It was a point of pride and dogma that they were not fighting for material rewards, but stood for patriotism and humanity against the imperial tyranny of Argentina.

Unfortunately, the cause was not worthy of its champion, nor were the members of the government at Montevideo as disinterested as Garibaldi himself. Behind the lines divergent factions struggled for mastery in the capital. General Rivera himself was supplanted and exiled to Brazil. There was no single group, wrote home the British minister, whose political morality could be trusted, and many people were consequently leaving the country altogether. Rivera had been more humane than his rivals, and perhaps better disposed towards the foreign commerce upon which the republic depended. But against him was "his notorious bad faith, his want of probity in the appropriation of the publick money, the unscrupulous means which he has always employed to sustain an illegitimate influence in the Republick". It was a choice between the devil and the deep sea.

Plagued by internal divisions, in the summer of 1845 the government opened negotiations to win the active support of France and England, and these two

powers finally intervened to defend their interests and
guarantee Uruguayan independence against the Argentine. In August, Garibaldi, closely in conjunction with
French and British naval units, began to push the
enemy back from their siege of the city. At the same
time he privately sought to negotiate with some of
the enemy commanders and find some peaceable solution to a tragic and fruitless war, for he thought it
could be safely assumed that this foreign intervention was dictated by other interests than those of the
local inhabitants.

Failing with these surreptitious negotiations, he
drove as far inland as he could find a navigable river,
still accompanied by French and British detachments.
He was also helped by an Irishman, Joseph Mundell,
who recruited a local militia and used it for acts of
brigandage. The going was not easy. His men often had
to live on horseflesh, and they were obliged to levy
a substantial and unpopular toll in money and provisions on the countryside as they went. Some of
the Italian Legion mutinied again in December, but
the main body covered themselves with glory. Garibaldi later claimed that in a hundred fights along the
Rio de la Plata he had not known a single defeat.

Their most celebrated passage of arms was in
February 1846 by the river Sant'Antonio. He was
marching his small unit of about two hundred and
fifty to make contact with the main Uruguayan army,
when the enemy deceived him into accepting battle
against a force four times as strong. His cavalry fled
away and the remnant had to keep up a continual fire
from midday until they could escape under cover of
darkness. It was a victory for courage and endurance under a blazing sun with no water to drink.
The bodies of men and horses were made into a ram-
part, and mortally wounded men were inspired to go

on fighting. Thirty were killed and many more wounded, and the exhausted remainder then had to face a four-hour march to their camp. Garibaldi proudly boasted that he would not give up membership in the Italian Legion for a world of gold, and ostentatiously refused promotion at the price of so much Italian blood.

In the same month, February 1846, the balance of power at Montevideo changed once again, and a *coup d'état* brought what was left of parliamentary government to a stop. This persuaded many of the landowners that the exiled Rivera might have to be recalled once again to restore stable government. With this much encouragement, the ex-president furtively returned to watch the development of events from the safe distance of a ship in the harbour. In April an insurrection was instigated among the troops, and he was invited ashore to quell it. Once in command, he reappointed his friends to all important military and civil posts, and the counter-revolution was complete.

Garibaldi adhered to the new régime, as the cause of Uruguay was still "good and generous"; but he acted more reluctantly now, because it looked less and less like a war for liberty and patriotism. He had to write and complain that these city politics made everyone forget even to supply the army with food and reinforcements. As so often in his life, politics interfered with the fighting and he therefore liked politics the less. His conduct of the war also suffered from the interference of diplomacy, for England and France were now calling the tune, and their fiat alone stood between the republic and invasion by Rosas. There was less honour now to be had in serving such a cause, less chance of any other signal feat of arms.

The British minister at Montevideo reported to

Lord Palmerston that Garibaldi continued to show "great skill and bravery", and that, while the government was full of corruption and venality, never the least sign of peculation was found in the subsidy paid to the Italian Legion. Garibaldi was, as he always remained, a man of complete integrity, though his family was living a threadbare existence, his own few clothes were tattered, and his pay and rations were invariably behindhand.

For a while longer he hesitated to make a public admission of his disillusionment. His credulousness could always take a deal of stretching, and his heroic and romanticized idea of life was not easily undermined. He did not yield at once even when in 1847 he saw Rivera defeated in yet another campaign by Oribe and again leave for exile in Brazil. The political situation changed and changed about, but the defence of the capital went on.

Such a foreign upstart from Italy was, of course, not very popular among the native officers aspiring to high command in Montevideo. Nor was he popular with the European merchants whose goods he impounded on the plea of preserving the blockade, and who therefore complained against him to the government. Nor did he retain the full confidence of the French and British auxiliary forces. The European diplomats had concluded that the war was being artificially fanned by rival factions in the city, and that only a compromise peace with Argentina could guarantee the continued independence of Uruguay. Under their advice, the party in power began to negotiate for such a compromise peace; but the Italian Legion in August 1847 turned out under arms to protest against this proposal, and some of the ministers were forced to resign. It seemed to outside observers that Garibaldi and his Legion were becoming just

C

one more of the factions, either from dull-wittedness, or because they were being exploited by other concealed interests, or else because the legionaries feared to be out of a job if peace were restored.

As the diplomats were now firmly in charge, under their influence the war tailed off to an anticlimax. There was discord in the Italian Legion; its numbers were diminishing as the future became more uncertain, and some elements were still opposed to Garibaldi's command. It was time for him to look back at events in Italy and to search out other fields to conquer where the cause of justice was more manifestly at issue and his own presence more obviously welcome.

CHAPTER FOUR

REVOLUTION AND ROME

1848-1849

GARIBALDI had not forgotten Italy during these years of exile. He had kept in touch with Mazzini, and had even offered to bring six hundred men over to Europe for a revolutionary war if only Mazzini could find the necessary means. Though the money could not be found, the republicans in Italy were none the less vastly proud of his exploits in America. So even were some of the monarchists, and in 1846 a few of them contributed to send him out a sword of honour. Between two such dogmatic political opposites he himself had now learned to trim his sails just a little, for politics were not to be allowed to stand in the way of his return home. Simultaneously he tried to make up his quarrel with Mazzini's great enemy, King Charles Albert of Piedmont, and vainly petitioned to receive a pardon for his criminal conspiracy of 1834.

The years 1846-1848 were tremendously exciting to Italian patriots and liberals because the Pope and the rulers of Naples, Tuscany, and Piedmont were all being induced to grant constitutional and economic reforms. In 1847 Garibaldi, under the influence of this excitement, went so far as to write a respectful and filial letter offering the services of himself and his Legion to Pope Pius IX. When the Vatican did not reply he made a similar attempt to enter the employ of the Grand Duke of Tuscany. By now he was determined to return somehow, and Anita was sent on ahead with their three children to look after his mother in Nice while he in Montevideo set about collecting the necessary money to finance the journey.

Finally, in April 1848, he was able to set out on the two-month passage home to Italy. Only sixty of his six hundred eventually decided to come with him, two of these being Negroes Garibaldi had helped to liberate. The ship also carried the mortal remains of his dead daughter Rosita, which he had privily dug up by night from the cemetery so that he might take them back for burial with his ancestors. During the long journey home a bad fire nearly destroyed the ship with all hands. Every evening aboard, these hardened warriors sang together a patriotic hymn at sundown. But it was now an Italian song that they sang, not the Uruguayan hymn that had kept up their spirits during the Battle of Sant'Antonio. They were returning for the resurrection, or *risorgimento*, of Italy.

It was a great day when Garibaldi landed at Nice after all these long years, especially as Charles Albert had just declared war on Austria and the long-awaited hour of national redemption seemed at hand. His ship

was flying the Montevidean flag lest the sentence of
death from 1834 should still be preferred against him.
But popular excitement swept away even the usual
quarantine regulations. At a banquet in his honour
at the Hotel New York he spoke (in French) of his
hope that the Austrians might be thrown right out of
the Italian peninsula before the end of the year. It
was noted that he took care to speak well of the King,
and not to pose as a pure republican of Mazzini's
school.

Emboldened and stimulated by his reception,
Garibaldi again offered to enlist under Charles Albert.
He marched to the royal headquarters, but there a
chilly interview damped his enthusiasm, and the King
privately stated his opinion that to employ this ex-
pirate and convict would dishonour the army. The
Piedmontese bureaucrats were ignorant of his deeds
in America, while the politicians distrusted his radicalism and the generals despised his lack of regular
military training. Few of the Piedmontese soldiery
had seen any active service, let alone as much as
Garibaldi, but they had been to the right military
academies and studied the right textbooks, and their
mixture of jealousy and disdain was to pursue him all
the rest of his life. They now told him to go off and ply
his trade of corsair in the Adriatic.

Once this offer to fight for Piedmont was refused,
the suspicion began to grow, and with some reason,
that Charles Albert was not fighting Austria out of any
exalted feeling of Italian patriotism. His chief motive
was said to be that of enlarging his own petty kingdom of Piedmont at the expense of Milan and Venice;
and his secondary motive was to prevent or control
any popular and republican outburst in the rest of
northern Italy. Neither intention did the King much
credit in the eyes of good radicals and patriots.

Garibaldi therefore betook himself to Milan, which had risen independently of Piedmont and single-handed had driven out its Austrian garrison. Here he was met with bands and parades, and Mazzini himself was carrying a banner when he inspected the troops. Forced to make a speech, Garibaldi thanked the people for their ovation, but added that it was no time for applause and talk. Applause there was to be in plenty, but not much active help in the way of weapons and supplies, and although Garibaldi himself was made a general, his men had to make do with converted Austrian uniforms. He was greatly excited all the same, for "liberation of one's country from the foreigner is the most beautiful, the most sublime thing possible"; at last here was a cause worthy of his mettle. Then suddenly, after a week of great expectations, Charles Albert's not very efficient army was defeated at Custoza and withdrew from the war. The position of Milan by itself was rendered untenable.

As so often in the past, Italians had again proved to be divided among themselves, monarchists from republicans, Turin from Milan, regulars from volunteers. The Piedmontese had expected to be welcomed as deliverers; instead, the peasants of Lombardy had sometimes opened the dikes and flooded the land against them. Garibaldi in his memoirs lamented that the Italians were not so unified as even the hybrid people of Rio Grande, nor so morally strong in adversity; "otherwise the foreigner would no longer trample your soil, and you would have regained your position among the great powers of the world".

Charles Albert not only retreated, but also ordered Garibaldi to demobilize. The latter, however, claimed his right as a free citizen to continue the fight alone, especially as his allegiance was to Milan and not at all to Turin. Although the general demoralization had spread to his own men, he defied the King's order for his arrest and fell back on Mazzini's doctrine of popular insurrection. In despair, he called on people to take up a scythe or a stick and somehow make the armistice impossible. He publicly referred to the Piedmontese as cowards and traitors who had only intervened in the war to ensure that it could not result in a political victory for the republicans.

For about twelve days Garibaldi kept a small war going by himself. With a thousand men he seized several paddle-steamers on Lake Maggiore and penetrated Austrian territory. In at least one encounter he actually carried the day in a pitched fight. But it was a futile business, except as a moral protest against a stigma on Italians which he now imagined to exist. Wherever he went, he had to levy a tithe of money and food on the inhabitants, a practice that cannot have increased his popularity. The right to do so he claimed in virtue of "having been elected in Milan by the people and their representatives to be a *duce*". These same people, nevertheless, would not now join him. Information about the enemy could often not even be bought at a price, while the Austrians readily found spies and traitors among the very Lombards whom he had hoped would rise in insurrection.

A description of Garibaldi's tactics would have to be given in great detail to be accurate. Any simplification would tend to distort the perspective and make insufficient allowance for the paramount importance of chance and accident. More interesting is the fact that these few days at least showed Garibaldi that he could apply the lessons of South American warfare to conditions in Italy. Fast-moving, with little baggage, his small units could dissolve quickly into the countryside and then come down unexpectedly from the hills to cut lines of communication. He knew that, in certain conditions, volunteers defending their own land could stand up to a regular army. What they lacked in training might be more than made up in the ferocity, desperateness, and endurance with which they would fight for their own. At the moment, however, conditions were unfavourable; apparently the common people were as ready to defend their land against the revolutionary nationalists as against their foreign overlords.

By the end of August, Garibaldi's numbers were down to about thirty, and utterly exhausted and with malaria upon him, he finally had to escape across the lake into Switzerland disguised as a peasant. His failure struck a wounding blow at the Mazzinian assumption that the common people were eager to rise for the cause of nationalism. The Austrian empire, far from being on the point of disintegration as Mazzini had said, had put down the Italian revolt with consummate ease. Instead of being a fine protest, this first war of liberation had been worse than useless, for it had weakened Italian morale and opened up wider internal divisions. "All the weaknesses of our character had been revealed . . . all the results of our rhetorical education and our soft and anti-military way of life."

In September 1848 Garibaldi was allowed to return to Nice, despite his angry disobedience of the King. We find him once again speaking to the mob from his favourite stance on a balcony, this time at San Remo. In October, to Mazzini's disgust, he was elected one of the Ligurian deputies to the Turin parliament, though he never in fact took his seat. An election address described himself as "the representative of the people": he had nothing but his sword to offer them, he said, but it was dedicated to their service. This was unparliamentary language, but Garibaldi was himself deceived by rhetoric more easily than he would have liked to think. Applause and votes there were abundantly, but this did not necessarily mean that people were willing to sacrifice and suffer; they might be ready to employ his sword, but not necessarily to unsheathe their own.

Clearly, he was now fixed in general opinion as a highly colourful personality, to some extent above the law, a man whose genuine altruism and real courage and ability and panache shone obviously amid the deceits and treasons of the time. His proclamations, call them lapidary or vapid as you will, had a calculated appeal and do not sound wholly false. "Put not your trust in princes but in your own right arm. Whoever has the will to conquer, will conquer." It was something to be so single-minded and simple-minded.

As the war in Lombardy was over, Garibaldi chartered a vessel and left with seventy men for Sicily, which was up in arms against the Bourbon government of Naples. This was on a sudden whim and without a word of explanation even to his friends. En route to the south he was taken by another such whim and stopped off at Florence, hoping to obtain command of the troops of insurrectionary Tuscany against the King of Naples. He therefore wooed "this most intelligent and civilized of the peoples of Italy", and held out the tempting bait that Florence might become the national capital. From this new centre he summoned all Italians to rise against the barbarians in a pitiless war of national vendetta.

But the bait was not sufficiently attractive. Even the popular and revolutionary government of Tuscany was uneasy with this firebrand so near. He was not given any military appointment, and even had to rely on private contributions to feed his private army. Only when he expressed his willingness to fight instead for Venice against Austria did the Florentine government make it easy for him to recruit more volunteers, delighted to be so cheaply rid of a nuisance who might prove dangerous as well as expensive. For himself, he was determined upon action of some sort somewhere, if not in Sicily or Tuscany then in Venice, and he continued to issue stirring appeals full of generalized patriotic clichés and exclamation marks.

His followers were by this time a mixed bunch, some of them idealists thinking of a united Italy, others quarrelsome and factious. Few came from his native Liguria, and there were almost no Piedmontese or southerners. One company was to consist of boys between twelve and fifteen years old. Probably most were people who, for political or other reasons, had to lead a wandering existence, with nothing to lose and all to gain from a life of violence. Some few had been with him in America and wore Gaucho costume, people who would lasso stray animals for food and barbecue them in the open. Hardly any wore red shirts, for they still despised anything like a uniform as too typical of the regular soldiery.

At the end of 1848 this makeshift army had to cross the Apennines several times in the bitter cold. On the way northward to Venice they heard of the assassination of the Pope's minister Rossi, and though Garibaldi was no enthusiast for political assassination, he welcomed this particular act and it helped decide him to turn southward to Rome. This minister's assassination persuaded the Pope to take immediate refuge with the King of Naples. This sudden act of abdication added Rome to the list of revolutionary cities.

Everywhere on the way south they were met with music and much kissing; but again it was a skin-deep enthusiasm. They looked too much like just another group of brigands. When Garibaldi arrived at Rome he was given the rank of colonel but not the post of

commander-in-chief as he had hoped, and his men
had to move out into the countryside, where their
existence would be cheaper and their presence less
frightening. No one could have guessed that the heroic
defence of the Roman republic during the next few
months was to make Garibaldi's name familiar throughout Europe.

In January 1849 he was elected by Macerata as a
delegate to the Roman assembly, but had to be carried
into the Assembly Hall because of arthritis contracted
up in the wind-swept Apennines. There on the Capitol,
impetuous as ever, he was the first to raise his voice
for the constitution of a Roman republic. His several
speeches at this time show him an uncompromising
republican and a believer in a unified Italian state,
though by no means everyone was ready to follow him
so fast or so far.

His experiences in the assembly are enough to
show how inexperienced he was and how unsuited to
any form of parliamentary government. It irked him
that people should orate so much and do so little. The
deputies processed formally through the streets, with
tricolour bands over their frock coats; and inside the
chamber, too, their first instinct was to insist on the
due observance of forms, for they felt the importance
of the occasion in their own way. Garibaldi told them
that the people were not interested in forms, only in
decisions and actions; but he was snubbed and over-
ruled, and his own conclusion was that in future he
ought to appeal directly to the people and not merely
to their elected representatives in parliament.

In March 1849 Piedmont made a desultory attempt
to renew the war against Austria and so recover her
leading position in Italy. Garibaldi, still idle and
champing for action, again offered to join in with his
volunteers, but after only a few days the defeat of

Novara forced Charles Albert to surrender and abdicate. Tuscany, too, withdrew from the revolution and invited the Grand Duke back to his throne. Only Rome, Venice, and Sicily retained for a while longer their revolutionary independence.

Mazzini arrived at Rome in March and was elected by the assembly as one of the Triumvirs with full powers to conserve the republic. Until April, Garibaldi still had to hold his volunteer army some miles out at Rieti. Technically he had been permitted to keep only five hundred under arms, but in fact had over a thousand. Hence, funds were insufficient, so that the volunteers sometimes resorted to thieving and made themselves a general nuisance. He grumbled to the Triumvirs that he could not pay the partisans under his command, and touchily complained that the republican government was not properly using the skill that he had learned in a hundred battles. He resented the fact that his true worth was being concealed behind such epithets as "pirate, smuggler, or guerrilla", and he once threatened to resign altogether if they did not apologize for these insults. The common people were too firmly attached to their religion to be very enthusiastic about the republic, but he was sure that his personal prestige with them was high, and he demanded full powers to roam with his men at will through Italy to work up enthusiasm for the war. This was to protest too much. Obedience did not come easily to Garibaldi, and he was in danger of earning a reputation for pique and arrogance and unreliability.

At the end of April, Avezzana, who had returned from the United States to be minister of war, appointed Garibaldi a general and called him in to help with the defence of Rome. Avezzana later claimed special credit for this, as many people had been frightened of such a dangerous character and had begged that he be kept well away. But there was a serious emergency to meet, as Louis Napoleon had just landed a detachment of French soldiers in order to defeat the republic and restore the Pope. On April 30 a French attack was beaten off with many casualties, to the great surprise of the attacking force. General Avezzana was in charge of the defence, but Garibaldi particularly distinguished himself in a sharp clash among the spring flowers on the Janiculan Hill. Although wounded, he was anxious to follow up the victory, and had to be restrained by the Triumvirate, who still hoped that republican France could be persuaded into neutrality. In fact, Louis Napoleon had too much need of the Catholic vote in France to be able to put republicanism before religion, and, in any case, he was already planning to abolish the French republic and crown himself Emperor; he was determined to ingratiate himself with the Catholics by capturing Rome.

After this engagement came a lull, the Garibaldians being mostly billeted in monasteries. In every sense of the word they were a force of irregulars, and we are told that the humour sometimes took them to parade with monkish cowls and candles. Other stories tell of sundry horseplay and of searching out love letters in a nunnery. They were soon moved out of Rome again to meet a threat from Naples, and early in May there was some fighting with the Neapolitans at Palestrina. Garibaldi claimed this as a victory, but so did General Lanza his opponent.

At Velletri occurred an unpleasant incident that nearly led Garibaldi into a duel. General Roselli had been appointed to the supreme command over Garibaldi because he was a Roman and because he was more dependable and disciplined. He was certainly a brave and conscientious soldier, but Garibaldi, who had more experience, resented this appointment. He clearly disobeyed Roselli's orders by provoking an engagement at Velletri. This was justified by success, though the success was not nearly so great as was claimed. Garibaldi's own habit was always to press on without counting the cost—often, it seems, without counting even the rough strength of the enemy; he aimed at continued surprise, constant aggression, at always keeping the initiative and following up any success. And this made him too independent to be a good subordinate.

Hence also arose many of his differences with Mazzini and the civilians at Rome. While Garibaldi took a large view of the revolution, Mazzini, with his almost mystical idea of Rome as the pulsating heart of Italy, wanted concentration on defence of the city. He thus summoned an unwilling Garibaldi back from pursuing the Neapolitans, because a Spanish army was now at Gaeta and the Austrians were moving up in the centre, so that four armies were forming up against the insurgents. The French had raised their numbers from 6,000 to 20,000 and, instead of being inferior in numbers, now had a superiority of more than two to one. Garibaldi wrote peremptorily to Mazzini that he wanted to stay out of Rome and work up a fast-moving guerrilla war in the mountains: if he had to remain in the city, it could be only as either a dictator with full powers or a simple soldier without any responsibility of command. Mazzini replied in desperation that everywhere he found distrust and division, and Garibaldi for the moment gave up his threat and took his place in the defence.

Garibaldi was a great believer in dictatorial powers, and in later years caustically reproached Mazzini for having lacked both the qualities of a dictator and courage to assume the title. "When your ship is in danger of being wrecked, you must boldly seize the helm," he said in his customary nautical metaphor. He also blamed the Triumvirs for not taking advice from their military experts, and for not following any single line of conduct without second thoughts and faltering. Mazzini, with equal or superior justice, taxed Garibaldi with disobedience, factiousness, and trying to desert the ship while it was sinking. The general had been peevish, argumentative, and full of absurd suscepti- bilities, and his protests and threats had made Maz- zini's task no easier. These two men, with so much in common, from now onward could never quite under- stand each other. Their natures were too imperious and inflexible to live together amicably.

The main French attack began on June 3, and during a month of siege the republic just held out. For the more exciting incidents there are a number of discrepant accounts to reconcile, and the excitement can be adequately conveyed only by a detailed analysis of the tactical to-and-fro; but there the English-speak- ing reader has G. M. Trevelyan's fine narrative as his guide. The odds were hopeless against the defenders, few in number, ill-armed and half-trained as they were, and handicapped by the passive indifference of nearly all the Romans except perhaps the inhabitants of Trastevere. But the heroism of these volunteer soldiers from most parts of Italy, coupled with Mazzini's will- power and Garibaldi's flair, helped to make a lost cause into one that ultimately won. It can be called a moral victory, if only because it accustomed Europe to think that Rome must belong one day to Italy and not to the Vatican. In 1870 the harvest was reaped which had been sown in blood twenty-one years earlier.

Garibaldi dominated the whole defence with an infectious self-confidence. It was a triumph of mind over matter. Yet his tactics did not go uncriticized. On the very first day he determined to repel the French attack at all costs, knowing how necessary it was to build up morale in his untrained troops. He repeatedly sent in his best men to capture and recapture the Villa Corsini, but only one unit at a time, and always with his favourite method of a frontal charge. Perhaps insufficient allowance was made for being up against better soldiers than he had ever known before. He had taken great pains to instruct his men in bayonet charges without firing, but these, while they worked against the volatile Neapolitans, were less effective against the steadier and hardened French. Nor did his previous training fit him for knowing how to use artillery in support of an attack on a strong point. The resultant loss of his best officers was very serious, as in this type of fighting everything might depend on leadership and experience. Many of the best-remembered names in the whole *risorgimento* were among those killed.

As late as June 25 Garibaldi believed that there was still hope. Rome, he said, had just written the finest page in modern history. But military weaknesses were becoming insistently obvious. Rôles were now reversed: Avezzana and Roselli wished to attack, and it was Garibaldi who decided that discipline and morale were too weak. Mazzini tartly criticized this caution, and complained of it tactlessly even to Garibaldi's own subordinates. One more rift was thus opened between these two radical leaders in a division that was to have important consequences for the future of Italy.

On June 30 a battle-weary and battle-stained Garibaldi was summoned to the Capitol, and the assembly rose to its feet in greeting. His sword was so bent that it would not properly sheathe. Asked his opinion, he gave it that no more defence was possible. And so it was agreed. At last Garibaldi was given the full powers he had asked, with permission to make his sortie and keep the revolution alive where he could.

On July 3 he left. The United States minister, Lewis Cass, offered him passage on a corvette, but this he refused though he took an American passport. About four thousand men were ready to go with him, and they met in the piazza before St. Peter's. All they could expect, he told them, was "heat and thirst by day, cold and hunger by night. You can hope for no wages but hard work and danger, without roof, without rest, just dearth and poverty, long night watches, long marches, and fighting at every step." Mazzini did not go with them but he too asked his friend and admirer the American minister for a passport, and was issued one under the false name of George Moore. Neither did Medici go, nor did many others who had fought most bravely for Rome, as, from any realistic viewpoint, the war was over. Italian independence, to say nothing of Italian unity, was still to seek.

CHAPTER FIVE

ESCAPE AND EXILE

1849-1854

GARIBALDI'S spectacular retreat from Rome is a fitting postlude to the tragedy of 1849 in Italy. He seems to have left the city with real hope that he could still make a fine war of it. When this expectation failed, his next thought was to keep a last stronghold for the revolution in the marshes and mountains of central Italy; and then he fell back on the idea of embarking upon some floating republic in the Adriatic and sailing to wherever freedom was at issue with tyranny. He always believed in fortune, and indeed fortune usually was on his side; but during the month of July, on the arduous and harassed march to San Marino, these fine hopes gradually deserted him. He had intended to break out from Rome and attack, but history has always called his march a retreat, and a retreat it was.

Though not open quite like other men to realistic considerations, Garibaldi could hardly help feeling disillusioned by the way things had gone. He had begun by trusting first the Pope and then Charles Albert, but each in turn had failed him. The Piedmontese army had twice been decisively beaten, and Lombardy, Tuscany, and Naples had successively hauled down the flag of revolution. Austria, the Papalists, and the old local dynasties of Italy had triumphed. He was even at odds with Mazzini, who he felt had let him down; and, to crown all, the common people, from whom he had expected so much, were unenthusiastic if not actively opposed to the revolution. In despair he had written to his wife, Anita:

"How you must despise this hermaphrodite generation of Italians, these countrymen of mine whom I have often tried to ennoble, little though they deserve it. The fact is that treachery has paralysed every generous movement. We have been dishonoured, and the name of Italian will be a laughing-stock for foreigners in every country. I am disgusted to belong to a family of so many cowards."

Anita had joined him at Rome during the last days of the siege. Now that he was a fugitive again, she insisted on riding at his side, although she was about five months pregnant and her presence must often have

D

been an embarrassment. She cut off her magnificent black hair and dressed in man's clothes as an officer as they rode off on what was to prove her last journey.

As they left Rome it was known that they would have to run the gauntlet of Austrian, French, Spanish, and Neapolitan armies. Occasionally the cities through which they passed gave them a royal welcome and the cry was heard: "*Viva* Garibaldi, King of Italy!" But the local inhabitants, even when they were kind and sympathetic, were never tempted to join this profitless expedition, and some towns pointedly barred their gates. Under the full powers recently granted at Rome, Garibaldi claimed authority to requisition supplies, preferably from the rich and from monasteries, but also if necessary from the peasants. Small wonder that this wandering horde were sometimes looked upon as marauders and met with gunfire. Garibaldi imposed the death penalty as summarily for theft as he did for cowardice, and we are told that he would shoot a man without stopping to take the cigar out of his mouth; but he could not prevent deserters from stealing and terrorizing the countryside under false pretence of being his rearguard.

Desertion was the chief problem. Although at Terni he was joined by a well-trained auxiliary force under the Englishman Colonel Forbes, every night many others stole off into the darkness, for it was increasingly difficult to detect any positive aim in their shiftless course and Garibaldi could not impart that sense of constant success on which he usually relied to give his men the will to win. After six days his four thousand were twenty-five hundred. He noted sadly that it was the officers especially who deserted, some of whom had been his companions ever since they had fought together in South America. They had the wit to recognize a lost cause when they saw one.

There was no hope for it, and on July 31 Garibaldi decided to accept temporary asylum in the neutral republic of San Marino, laying down his arms and dissolving his army. He and some two hundred and fifty others then fled through the Austrian ranks by night, and after nearly twenty-four hours of marching reached the Adriatic. There they embarked, but a further twist of fate brought it about that most of the boats were overtaken and captured in vivid moonlight. Some of the prisoners were executed, and among these was Ugo Bassi, the red-shirted Barnabite who had acted as chaplain to the Legion. Garibaldi himself escaped to the shore, where he was lucky enough to fall in with some of Mazzini's adherents, who took care of him through their underground network.

Anita was now dangerously ill, overwhelmed by exhaustion in the burning heat, but although Garibaldi wanted to leave her in safety she again insisted on accompanying him. Disguised as a labourer, he led her along in a cart under a sunshade, and in the desolate marshland of the Romagna on August 4 she died. Subsequent patriotic hagiology, confronted with the difficult task of discovering a heroine in the saga of national revival, conferred on this South American woman a posthumous beatification. She was a fine and courageous person, but never quite lived up to her legend.

There was time only for a hurried burial in the loose sand. With the Austrians close on his heels, Garibaldi spent the next month escaping back across the peninsula. He was passed on from house to house, over swamps and marshes, sometimes eating in the same café as the soldiers who were searching for him. Many humble but brave citizens were moved by admiration and sympathy to help his passage, and once a priest carried this infidel outlaw over a stream in flood. He had no money, but was never allowed to starve, and no one betrayed him. And finally, on September 2, he reached safety on a ship off the Tuscany coast.

The government in Turin was not exactly delighted at his arrival home. Indeed, at the frontier it had been ordered that none of the defenders of Rome, and especially not himself, should be allowed to enter Piedmontese territory, and a public statement was made to the effect that by fighting at Rome he had forfeited his rights of citizenship. The defence of Rome, however, had made him a general hero, and the government dared not be too stern. He was arrested, though always treated with consideration, and in the end they decided to send him back to America. There was a particular hurry because the parliamentary elections were due to take place on September 16 and it was important that Garibaldi should not be elected. Moreover, a majority vote in parliament decided that his arrest and expulsion were a violation of the constitution. He himself was kept quiet by the promise of a pension to maintain his family. For one single day he was allowed to visit his relatives, on the strict condition that he sought no publicity. He took leave of his mother, whom he was never to see again, and his children were boarded out with friends. Then he departed for another four years of frustration and exile.

Garibaldi could not guess that he would be gone four years. As he had a lively hope that Italy would need him soon, he did not want to travel too far afield, and there were political reasons why he did not wish to return to Montevideo. So long as he went somewhere abroad, the government did not much mind. On September 19 he arrived at Tunis in a Piedmontese gunboat, but the Bey would not let him land, so he was taken back to the island of Maddalena, where he

spent a few tranquil days fishing, hunting, and playing bowls. Meanwhile, the British government was
asked whether, "owing to the extreme difficulty of
removing General Garibaldi from the Sardinian states
in any other way", he might, as an emergency measure,
be allowed to stay on parole at Gibraltar. In later life
he grumbled that he had not been allowed to land at
Gibraltar either. In fact he arrived there and the
governor gave him permission to stay for a week until
a boat left for England; but Garibaldi replied that
he did not want to go on to either England or America.
The governor regretted that the fortress of Gibraltar
was no place for permanent political refugees, and
Tangier was suggested as an alternative.

"Here among the Turks I can live quietly," was
Garibaldi's acid comment when a ship of war deposited
him at Tangier. Luckily, he and several friends were
taken in by the Piedmontese consul, Carpenetti, himself also from Liguria, who proved an excellent companion for the next six months. The exile had been
allowed to bring his dog with him, and they all went
fishing and shooting together, often with Murray, the
British consul, as well. Hunting was Garibaldi's chief
exercise and pastime, and it always remained one of
his favourite occupations. He also spent long hours
making sails and fishing-tackle and cigars. And another
task that he began at Tangier was writing his memoirs.
He was anxious not to stir up too much mud and dissension about recent events, but he could at least tell
the story of his youth and career in South America.
This was the narrative that the American writer Theo-
dore Dwight published a few years later.

It was a boring existence to one who was so much
in love with action. Patiently but vainly he waited in
hope of another call to continue the good work of
national liberation. All he and his family at home had

to live on was a small pension from the government at Turin, for he never succeeded in securing the ship's captain job that he wanted. As time went by, he reluctantly concluded that he would have to try his fortune in the United States along with so many of his fellow countrymen. Only by obtaining American citizenship would he be able to sail under the American flag, and this seems to have been his intention.

In June 1850 he therefore left for the New World, sorrowfully leaving his dog behind with Murray to pine away and die. While at Liverpool on the way he was taken again with arthritis, so badly indeed that on his arrival in America he had to be carried ashore like so much luggage. This painful and gradually crippling ailment was to recur on and off for the rest of his life.

Soon after he reached New York a subscription was begun by some Italians to fit out a boat that he could command. Unfortunately, not nearly enough was collected, and he had to seek other employment. Failing to secure a position in the Post Office Department, he once tried to sign up as an ordinary seaman. Another Genoese, Meucci, then took him to work as a tallow-chandler. For several months he specialized in the making of candle wicks, being treated by his employer very much as one of the family and allowed to go fishing on Long Island when he wished. Apparently he sent what he could of his earnings back to his mother and children, just like any other Italian emigrant.

Perhaps the prospect of returning to Italy was receding as time went by and the Pope and the Austrians became ever more firmly entrenched. At any rate, during these nine months of 1850-1851 spent in the United States, he filed his intention to become a U.S. citizen and was given a passport. More than once in his life he was to claim American citizenship, but he never actually completed the formalities and his naturalization was not officially recognized.

In the spring of 1851 Garibaldi left with another Italian friend on a business trip to Peru, and a sailor he remained for the next three years. Very little is known of him during this time, for he wrote few letters and his life was mostly uneventful, unrecorded, and unmemorable. We may assume that he greatly increased his knowledge of the wide world and his experience as a leader of men. Jessie White, who saw much of him soon afterwards, gathered that this was the saddest period of his life, and he seldom spoke of it to his friends. He was farther away than ever from his children and country.

First he sailed down to Panama, where he was stricken again with malaria. He later described with some pride how at Lima he took up a quarrel with a Frenchman, "as I am somewhat intractable by nature", and searched him out at his home and drubbed him soundly; for there was a rankling grudge to pay off against France. In Peru he was given an independent command by another Genoese who had become rich in the silver mines. The *Carmen* was a square-rigged three-master, and he sailed her under the Peruvian flag, having become technically a Peruvian citizen so that he might take rank as a captain. Guerzoni, who was later to be Garibaldi's secretary and the confidant of many privately related incidents, says that its freight was grain, but no doubt this was a misreading of *grano* for *guano*.

In 1852 Garibaldi took the *Carmen* to the Far East, touching at Hong Kong, Canton, and Manila and coming back by Australia and New Zealand. During this voyage, so he says, he studied a book on winds and climate written in English. The language was one that, to his great regret, he never knew well, but he had begun to speak it a little in New York, and this subject of climatology was one in which he took particular interest. Before sailing, he had been in touch with observatories in America and had promised to send them any readings and information that he happened to discover.

He left Lima again on the same ship in 1853, this time rounding Cape Horn and sailing up to New York and Boston. Another four months were spent in the United States. Then he took over the three-masted *Commonwealth*, belonging to a wealthy Italian at Boston, and carried a cargo to England, thus returning to Europe after more than four years' absence. In this long while he had managed to improve his position and his fortune, and also to broaden his nautical experience, for these ocean-going vessels were much larger than the ships he had known in his youth. With the savings he had accumulated it was now possible for him to see if he could rejoin his family in Nice. As his mother had lately died, he ought to try and set up a home for his orphaned children.

CHAPTER SIX

PRIVATE LIFE

1854 - 1859

GARIBALDI arrived at London from America in February 1854, but only a few tantalizing flashes illuminate his short visit. Most dramatic of all, this rugged sea dog was to become engaged to a rich society widow, a certain Mrs. Roberts. Another fascinating but unrecorded interview took place when the United States consul invited him to dinner along with the future President Buchanan. London was the great asylum for international revolutionaries, so he also met not only Mazzini, but Kossuth the Hungarian, Herzen the Russian, and Ledru-Rollin the Frenchman. These encounters pitchforked him abruptly back into the world of politics.

Mazzini had written to Garibaldi, hoping that they could forget their past differences and agree to organize a republican revolt in Sicily. Personally they met on good terms. But Garibaldi was by now a little chary of Mazzini's high-handedness and rigid dogmatism. Herzen quotes Garibaldi as saying: "I know the Italian masses better than Mazzini does, for I have always lived among them. Mazzini knows only an intellectual Italy." And these Italian masses were certainly not ready for the ideal republic of Mazzini's dreams. In any case, it would be foolish to offend monarchical Piedmont while there was still a chance that all Italians, radical and conservative, might join together in a war of independence against Austria. National independence was what really mattered, not internal politics.

This was a more moderate, and statesmanlike Garibaldi than had been seen before. He urgently wanted permission to return home, and so was anxious not to give offence at Turin. The prime minister of Piedmont was now Count Cavour, the leader of the moderate liberals and an enemy of revolution. Cavour strongly disliked Mazzini and all his works, but always had a canny eye for prising away from the republican leader any dissident radicals who fell out with his leadership. Cavour was at first afraid to let Garibaldi return home, and even warned Britain against him lest more plans of Italian revolution were afoot. Only when it became clear that Garibaldi was not aiming for Sicily,

and on condition that he forgo politics, Cavour gave
permission for the exile to rejoin his family. Garibaldi
first left London for Newcastle, where the workers
presented him with another sword of honour; and then
took on a cargo of coal and sailed in April 1854 to
Genoa.

No sooner had he returned home than another
bout of rheumatism and arthritis forced him to take
a mud cure at Acqui. He rewarded Cavour by dis-
sociating himself from Mazzini and saying (so reported
the British minister) that in future he would fight only
for Piedmont. The Mazzinian newspapers were then
tactless enough to publicize Garibaldi's disobedience
at Rome in 1849. In replying to this attack, he steadily
refused to explain or refute the facts adduced, and
hoped to settle the matter simply by challenging
General Roselli to a duel. Angrily he wrote to the
papers warning Italian youth that Mazzini's policy
of continual insurrections only discredited the Italian
cause. In 1855, when Piedmont entered the Crimean
War on the side of France and England, Mazzini called
this a betrayal of Italian nationalism and advised
soldiers to desert, but Garibaldi stood with that branch
of radicalism which welcomed this attempt to make
the voice of Italy heard once again in Europe.

Mazzini was not altogether dismayed at these
signs of difference. He knew how changeable and
impetuous were the other's political views: "He will
never begin anything himself, but needs to be
presented with means already organized by others;
he will follow the republicans if we act first, or the
monarchists if they do." This analysis was not far
wrong. Republicans and monarchists were both a little
afraid of Garibaldi, yet both were soon competing
for his services; for even in retirement he was a marked
man.

It is typical of Garibaldi that he thought the peaceful domestic years 1854-1859 were of no interest in his life, but even their relative uneventfulness has a distinct concern to the outside observer. Most of 1854 he spent quietly at Nice, without occupying himself much or at all in politics. As he had been allowed home on sufferance, he had to go carefully, and was quite ready to wait and see if Cavour could offer an alternative programme of action to that of Mazzini's which he had found wanting. Regeneration might come about through quite unforeseen circumstances, he said, and perhaps quicker than most people thought.

One month he spent with Jessie White and his fiancée, Emma Roberts, on holiday in Sardinia. Sometimes there he used to shoot as many as several hundred birds a day, and the local grandees put on boar hunts for him. In 1855 he was again given his Master's Certificate by the government, and for a few months engaged in coastal trade once more. The Orlando brothers, that family of Sicilian radicals who were founding in Liguria the great naval-armament firm of Ansaldo, gave him command of the *Salvatore*, the first screw-propelled steamer to fly the Italian flag.

The first impression Garibaldi made on Miss White was as "a simple courteous gentleman, of few words, and shy of going into society". He always rose at dawn, and even when at home in Nice went out most mornings to shoot partridges or even to shoot fish. He slept after lunch, and went to bed at eight each night. He hated social engagements. When expected out to dinner he would sometimes just not turn up at all, but go off at the last minute to play bowls. He was also a great player of draughts and seldom lost, but would never try chess, for he said it took less time to become a good general than a good chess-player. He sometimes listened to music, for Mrs. Roberts was an accomplished pianist, but he seemed to enjoy it only when she struck up some patriotic tune.

Garibaldi was now nearing fifty and wanted to settle down. His arthritis unfitted him for a seafaring life. His motherless children had been living with friends who acted as guardians. When, in the autumn of 1855, his brother Felice died and left him a sum of money, this together with his savings enabled him to set up house on his own. As with many other Italians who had made good in the New World, to buy a small farm in his native land was a natural instinct, and eventually he fixed on the desolate island of Caprera, where some plots of land were up for sale very cheaply.

Caprera was situated in the rocky archipelago of Maddalena, between Corsica and Sardinia. On the remote horizon were Elba and that other romantic island, Monte Cristo. Maddalena itself had been familiar territory to Nelson, and Garibaldi himself had already lived there for a short while. It was a sailor's choice to select somewhere so solitary and free, in the middle of wild nature, and where there was no government or rule to obey. Dumas tells us that when Garibaldi had sailed past the Juan Fernández Islands in the South Pacific he had called Robinson Crusoe the happiest man in the world. It was an early dream come true.

One boat a month came to Maddalena from Genoa; otherwise, Caprera was isolated except for the eagles hovering over its indented rocky shores and the wild goats from which it took its name. Most of the island was barren granite, wild and steep, torn by wind and waves. "It is difficult to realize the pleasures of a spot where man has never fixed his abode," said Vecchi, "such is its profound peace and unbroken silence."

Garibaldi was able to buy half the island in 1855. The rest belonged to a Mr. Collins, an eccentric and

unsociable Englishman who for about twenty years
had lived with his wife in a hut on Maddalena. One
legend was that Collins had sailed with Nelson;
another was that his wife was a rich lady and he had
been her groom; in any case, they were an unneigh-
bourly couple, and their animals were always breaking
into Garibaldi's garden. Years later some other Englishmen bought Collin's half of the island and gave it to
Garibaldi as a present.

Caprera was oblong, about four miles by three.
Several families of shepherds had lived there in huts
and natural grottoes. There was one sizable hill with
a splendid view that Garibaldi would contemplate
silently for hours on end. It was a dry and barren
island, very windy, but with a temperate climate and
healthy air. Rough bushes, brambles, juniper, and
myrtle grew in the ledges and interstices of the rock,
and Trevelyan later noticed rock rose, tamarisk,
lavender, and asphodel. There was one spring of fresh
water in the centre. No proper harbour for boats
existed, and there were shoals and reefs everywhere;
but fish abounded, so Garibaldi could indulge in one
of his most absorbing hobbies.

For the first eighteen months Garibaldi was at
Caprera only on occasional visits. Three or four old
companions in arms, together with his son Menotti,
now aged fifteen, helped him build a house with local
granite and wood brought from Nice, and meanwhile
they all lived under canvas. The White House, or Casa
Bianca, was a one-floor building in the Montevidean
style, with four rooms and a flat roof to catch water.
Garibaldi proved to be a bad mason, and soon was
employed only in carrying the stones. An expert brick-
layer and carpenter had to be brought in to go over his
work and supervise the technical business of construction.

This was the place that Garibaldi gradually turned into a farm, with cows, horses, pigeons, poultry, and bees. He built a garden and paths. He planted cereals and root vegetables where he could find enough earth, and sometimes had first to plant the earth itself. Elsewhere he grew apples, peachesfi pears, almonds, even sugar cane, for he hoped to make himself quite self-sufficient. He had to bore wells, and before long was to need a windmill and a steam engine for pumping water.

The expense of all this was in the long run to prove considerable, for the island was as sterile as it was wild and beautiful; but luckily his friends abroad sent a constant succession of gifts in money and kind. Visitors, too, became increasingly frequent. Signora Deidery was there often, an elderly lady who took charge of his favourite daughter, Teresita, and tried to mitigate the boredom felt by this high-spirited girl in such a lonely place. A few other friends were always at Caprera, either working outdoors or acting as secretaries in dealing with the enormous amount of mail which came for him in later years (the number of unstamped letters arriving was to be a drain on his always shaky finances, and he had to make public appeals about this through the Press, though he recouped a little by not stamping his own correspondence in reply).

Food was always plain at Garibaldi's table, and at first was not too plentiful. Thrushes and other birds were eaten salted and fried. There were dried vegetables, dried figs, raisins, and cheese. After two years, when Garibaldi brought in three shepherds under a share-cropping contract, he was listed as owning thirty head of cattle, a hundred sheep, and a hundred goats. But later he took more and more to vegetarianism, and the close contact with nature in solitude made him quite eccentric in his belief that animals and even vegetables had souls that should not be harmed. Along with his semi-vegetarianism, Garibaldi gave up liquor almost entirely, but retained an habitual fondness for cigars.

In 1856, before he had properly settled down in his new estate, Garibaldi visited England again to see Emma Roberts, to whom after two years he was still formally engaged. He also intended to use what remained of his brother's legacy to buy a cutter that he could sail between Caprera and civilization. Nor was a political motive wanting. A conspiracy was on foot which was abetted even inside the British Cabinet itself, aimed at releasing certain political prisoners whom the King of Naples had immured on the island of Santo Stefano. A ship, the *Isle of Thanet,* was bought for the purpose at Hull by the Director of the British Museum, and Garibaldi was to be its commander; it was wrecked off Yarmouth in October, however, and the project had to be dropped.

People noticed that this time Garibaldi did not call on Mazzini, though both were in London. But he did go to stay with Jessie White's father at Portsmouth, and "delighted the shipwrights by the knowledge he displayed of the smallest detail of their craft".

Back in Italy, he spent several months plying his new cutter from port to port with cargoes of wood and coal. This was the *Emma,* a small boat of some forty tons named after his benefactress and betrothed. The logbook of the *Emma* contains many mathematical jottings by Garibaldi, showing that he still retained an interest in problems of algebra and trigonometry and the like. When the ship was destroyed by fire in January 1857 his career as a sailor was ended. The White House was now ready, and, having no other means of livelihood, he settled down to the hard

business of agriculture which gave him such deep
satisfaction during the rest of his life.

For these ten years before 1859, Garibaldi was
having to twist his nature and live as a peaceful
citizen, and as a single person in possession of a
moderate competence he was clearly in want of a wife.
The engagement to Mrs. Roberts did not survive his
visit to England in 1856, and perhaps it had always
been a little improbable. She was a rich and talented
woman, but too rich and too talented for this rough-
hewn, anti-social recluse, and after two years her
children succeeded in breaking the match. Garibaldi
said afterwards that a month at her house would have
killed him, what with all the servants and late nights
and the dinners that lasted two or three hours. He
was altogether too unceremonious and unconventional
to like the delicate life of society.

Emma remained his friend, and sent him plants
and seeds for his garden, and also good advice about
becoming more temperate in politics. To her care he
entrusted his second son, Ricciotti. She took the boy to
England to be cured of a serious leg infection, and
he stayed on at school in Liverpool. Before long
Ricciotti had so far forgotten Italian that Garibaldi
jokingly commented on how little they could now
speak together.

Another woman who adored Garibaldi was the
Countess Maria Martini della Torre. She, too, met him
in London in 1854, but she was already married. Some
years later she donned the red shirt and followed him
into battle, ending her days in a madhouse.

A voluminous fan mail arrived from other ladies
and would-be ladies of every age and condition, for
the popular lion and celebrity then filled a need in
society which has since been met in other ways. Letters
of admiration and passion poured in especially from

England. It would not be too much to say that the
cause of Italian nationalism became popular in
England chiefly through the glamour and popularity
of Garibaldi, who in this way won an uncovenanted
but highly important political point for his country.
Among others, the Duchess of Sutherland and the wife
of Charles Seeley, M.P., wrote him letters that their
husbands would hardly have approved. In their eyes he
was a successful, romantic hero who treated women
as emancipated and always addressed them with a
most un-Victorian gallantry. Distance lent him a real
enchantment even in the eyes of so shrewd a woman as
Florence Nightingale, who was a regular contributor
to his funds.

It was a constant feature, this attraction towards
Garibaldi of rich, high-born women; but most of their
kind were disenchanted in the end because he turned
out to be rough and crude and without polish. The
women by whom he had children were all humble,
plebeian folk: Anita, and Battistina Ravello and
Francesca Armosino. Battistina was a sailor's daughter,
poor, ignorant, and not at all pretty. She went to
Caprera as a servant, and in 1859 bore him a daughter
whom he named after Anita and who became a wild
and untamable creature. It is said that he thought of
marrying Battistina in 1859, but there were at least two
other women whom he was seeking in marriage that
year. It was at this time that he went to disinter the
bones of his first wife, Anita, in order to secure a death
certificate that would free him for marrying again.

One of these two alternative candidates was the
elegant and beautiful Baroness Maria Espérance von
Schwartz. Probably she was, after Anita, the most
important woman in his life. Her father was a German
banker who had moved to England, and she was born
in London and passed as an Englishwoman. By 1857,

E

when she met Garibaldi, she had already lost one husband by suicide and another by divorce. Now thirty-six, she lived a cosmopolitan and dilettante existence as a writer of romantic novels and travel stories.

Espérance—or Speranza, as she became to Garibaldi—was probably in search of another adventure story when she visited Caprera in 1857. She was an intense, serious hero-worshipper, something of a faddist and more than a little neurotic. She had an idea that he might be persuaded to write more of his autobiography, which so far had been brought down only to 1848, and he did in fact contract with her to publish an expanded edition in German. She it was who travelled with him to the Romagna when he sought out the grave of his wife, and she also made an unsuccessful attempt to interest his fellow countrymen in raising a public subscription for a monument to the valiant and faithful Anita.

In 1858, on Speranza's second visit to Caprera, Garibaldi proposed marriage to her; and he proposed again in the following year, apparently without telling her of his daughter by Battistina Ravello. He was refused, and his interest thereupon flagged a little. Occasionally he favoured her by dictating some of his casual aphorisms or some poetry, especially, she said, when in one of his elegiac or patriotic moods. In 1859 she went at his request on a mission to Sicily to make contact with the revolutionaries. No doubt she exaggerated the importance of this mission, and he does not seem to have been impressed by the stories she told of her heroic conduct. She duly translated his memoirs into German; but suddenly at the end of 1859 he asked for his manuscript back, and, without answering her letters of protest, gave it instead to Alexandre Dumas for publication (and improvement) in French. Despite this treatment, even despite his sudden marriage in January 1860 to the Marchesina Raimondi, about which he had told her not a thing, Speranza von Schwartz remained Garibaldi's good friend, and took upon herself the education of his intractable daughter Anita.

As she was an intelligent if somewhat over-imaginative woman, Speranza's memoirs give us some interesting details of Garibaldi's life at Caprera. From her first visit, she described the half-hour walk from the landing-stage to the granite walls of the Casa Bianca. What she remembered particularly was Garibaldi's hunting-dogs, and the rusting, dusty relics of war, the flags and weapons from various countries which filled his own room. In the small library there were Shakespeare, Byron, Plutarch, and La Fontaine, and Arthur Young on agriculture, and other works in English on navigation and the art of war. In the garden he had already by 1857 cultivated vines, sugar cane, figs, and chestnuts, and she saw many charcoal pits smoking. He complained to her that the goats made it difficult to grow anything, and he was trying to get rid of them. It was a scene of industry and simplicity, and Garibaldi fitted exactly into his environment.

After her second visit the next year she added certain touches to the portrait. Garibaldi milked the cows himself. It was still his habit to go to bed promptly at sundown, and it was a very hard bed too. He spoke perfect French, she said, although he preferred his native Ligurian dialect. She noted that he was now wearing glasses to read the newspapers.

He was a fascinating puzzle to her, for he was more sophisticated than the bluff man of action she had anticipated. Yet his anecdotes showed that he retained a quite childlike mind, which would suddenly show itself in the middle of the most serious and important discussions. One is reminded of what Jessie White had discovered: that he did not have much sense of humour. Above all, he could neither laugh at himself nor allow others to do so. If she pulled his leg about a phrase he was overfond of, he would not speak to her all day. This is a side of Garibaldi's character that often went unobserved. The flatterers who usually insulated him from direct contact with normal life also tended to deceive him about himself, and the world at large was blinded to some of these deficiencies by his gracious and courteous bearing.

One strange thing that he told Speranza—it was in November 1858—was that he might go again to South America in the near future; and Sacerdote, the most recent and thorough of Garibaldi's biographers, confirms that the suggestion came once again from the Piedmontese government that he would be well advised to go off on his travels again. From this fate he was saved by the march of dramatic events.

CHAPTER SEVEN

THE NATIONAL QUESTION

1856-1859

IN the years 1859 and 1860 Garibaldi ceased to be what he had been in turn hitherto—sailor, pirate, farmer, radical revolutionary—and became the stylized national hero of countless historical textbooks.

He was now just over fifty. Late in 1859 the English minister, Hudson, called for a visit at Garibaldi's request, and his first impression was of a "soldierlike, broad-shouldered, deep-chested, thin-flanked man of 5 ft. 8, stepping lightly, and with a full mild hazel eye and a deep voice". His rough but expressive face had been bronzed and weathered in the open air—"indicating a most kind and generous heart", said John Bright after their first meeting. He had an open, courteous manner, with no evident presumption; yet along with a childish ingenuousness he had the imperious air of one used to commanding and being obeyed. He spoke little, but well. He was simple and straight and invited confidence, and possessed an inescapable fascination of personality.

Another Englishman who saw something of him in this year was the military attaché Colonel Cadogan. As Garibaldi was thought likely to have considerable influence in the future, it was important to know his quality, and careful comments were therefore sent back to the government at London. Cadogan, like others, was impressed by the real charm of manner and voice. A comparison was drawn with George Washington, as someone with great earnestness of purpose, great energy of execution, and a disinterested love of his country without personal ambition. Everyone commented on this appearance of magnanimous disinterestedness. Garibaldi was utterly sincere and possessed "a simplicity of character with almost childish illusions as to human nature". Again we have this reference to a childlike element in his make-up. The poorer classes already called him "*il padre d'Italia*", the father of his country. "His views, though broad and honest, hardly ever rise above the level of trite and popular generalities. But for this very reason perhaps he exercises an influence on his hearers which a more cultivated intelligence might fail to produce". The comment was incisive and just.

Garibaldi was not a remarkably complicated

character, but even in simple people a monolithic
integrity is sometimes clouded by rival and contradictory loyalties. By 1859 we can recognize that he
was, above all, a patriot who had learned from Mazzini
and his own conscience that the redemption of his
divided and backward country was the noblest of aims.
But almost equally he was an internationalist who
never let a local patriotism obscure his affection for
humanity at large. He had a deep admiration for other
countries, in particular for the United States, Great
Britain, and Switzerland; and his thoughts often ran
to projects for a United States of Europe and a utopian
condition of universal peace and brotherhood.

Another apparent contradiction was between an
increasing adherence to republicanism as the best form
of government, and a firm loyalty for most of his life
to the Piedmontese Crown. If the Royal House of
Savoy eventually triumphed over all possible alternative solutions to the Italian question—for example,
over republicanism and over a divided or federated
peninsula—this triumph was due to Garibaldi as much
as to any other man.

Underlying all the apparent contrasts is one constant fact: although Garibaldi often seemed unstable
and wrong-headed in practical politics, his fundamental principles were as firm as they were admirable.
An unvarying humanitarianism, an unmitigated love of
liberty and social justice, lay behind all his wars and
his politics. One would call him essentially a radical
and a democrat, and these terms describe something
typical and unalterable in his character. Mazzini spoke
of him as "the living incarnation of popular liberties".
To nobody did he use the deferential form of address,
Lei, excepting to King Victor Emanuel alone, and
whenever possible he positively forbade the degrading
habit of hand-kissing between men and the obsequious

use of honorific titles. All men were born free and equal in the sight of God.

He himself was the archetype of the common man; and common men from New York to Newcastle and Palermo recognized him at once as one of themselves, yet also as someone who had made good and thereby enhanced their own status. He therefore became almost literally their patron saint, and we even find a popular print showing a Garibaldi-Christ with his hand raised in blessing. The strong, benevolent features, with the hair cut *alla nazzarena,* all contributed to this illusion, and some of the peasants who saw him really believed that this was an avatar or a second advent.

The national movements of the nineteenth century had need of this type of transcendent, idealized yet strongly individualistic person. Garibaldi's notoriety and éclat proved to be an essential ingredient in winning over some of the common people to a national cause that otherwise would have seemed to them remote and profitless if indeed they understood it at all. The making of Italy was to prove a victory for the intellectuals, the liberals, the middle classes; not for the uneducated, who hardly knew what the word *Italy* meant; not for the poor, who felt its presence only in higher taxes and conscription; not for those who lost a paternal, protective ordering of society to gain a more grasping competitiveness in which the weaker went to the wall; not for the Catholic masses, who saw the Pope deprived of his temporal power and the monasteries dissolved and Church property confiscated. There can be little doubt that Garibaldi's prestige among ordinary people helped to obscure what was really happening until they were too late to resist it.

Likewise, the individualism of his views and actions was in practice a godsend to the cause of nationalism.

Though in retrospect Italian unification might seem planned and inevitable, in fact at the time there had been a great deal of touch-and-go; and, far from being carried out according to a plan or preconception, there had never been much co-ordination or intelligent direction from anyone. Therefore, Garibaldi's thoughtless taking of the law into his own hands without calculating the cost or the consequences had been invaluable; invaluable also was his uncritical but intuitive confidence, unshakable ever since 1849, that "Austria was a colossus of clay crumbling to bits". With such blind, unreasoning faith, and with the courage of his unreasonable convictions, a man might remove mountains or displace a frontier.

Cavour, on the other hand, who was later made out to have been the architect of national unification, had in fact been a sceptic until the eleventh hour. He needed the dangerous, irresponsible activity of people like Garibaldi to convince him that nationalism was practical politics. For Cavour was able to count the cost and be frightened by the dangers; whereas Garibaldi would start a revolution regardless, ready to be either disowned if he failed, or exploited by the government if he succeeded. Furthermore, when Cavour finally did become a nationalist, he was in a sense frightened into taking this step by the fear that Garibaldi and the radicals might monopolize nationalism and make it revolutionary in domestic as well as foreign policy. Cavour had to take over part of Garibaldi's programme if he wanted to retain his own premiership and keep Italy conservative.

Both Cavour and Garibaldi were necessary for the successful outcome of the events of 1859-60. These two wings of the national movement, conservative and radical, though continuing to distrust each other, were in fact brought together in a partial alliance. This was mainly the work of Daniele Manin, a Venetian exile in Paris, who founded the National Society to spread his doctrine that revolutionaries and monarchists should form a united front. Garibaldi joined this society, and Cavour kept in touch with it.

As early as 1854 Garibaldi was saying that he would no longer support casual Mazzinian revolutions unless they were backed by the Piedmontese monarchy. For Piedmont had an army forty thousand strong, and resources without which success would be problematical, and an ambitious King, whose desire to expand Piedmont might possibly be converted into a wish to create an altogether new nation of united Italy. Garibaldi therefore insisted that all factions must rally to Piedmont as the strongest single element in the peninsula. Though always remaining a convinced theoretical republican, he thought Italian society still too backward and corrupt for republicanism, and so was ready to give his absolute allegiance to King Victor Emanuel. This fact was of immense importance. Garibaldi's was already becoming a name to conjure with, and his adherence to the middle-of-the-road National Society was a decisive moment in Italian history.

Cavour's great design from 1856 onwards was a war against Austria. He wanted to capture for Piedmont the Austrian provinces of Lombardy and Venice and so unite at least northern Italy into a strong kingdom. For this purpose the Piedmontese army was too small; a popular rising and an army of volunteers would be a helpful addition; "he needed a popular name, and so tried to get hold of me". Garibaldi was thus summoned to Turin in August 1856. A witness of this their first meeting relates that Cavour was good-humoured and familiar, and gave Garibaldi to understand that great moves were afoot for the reconstruction of Italy if only the radicals would be patient and avoid any premature outbreak of revolt. This was enough to keep Garibaldi quiet when Mazzini and Pisacane engineered several abortive republican risings in 1857.

Again in August 1858 Garibaldi was called to Turin, and this time the messenger found him milking his cows on Caprera. These visits were among the few occasions in his life when he wore the conventional frock coat with top hat and stick, all borrowed from a friend at the last minute; before long he was too big a power in the land to have to observe such punctilio and etiquette. In December he saw Cavour yet again and heard more details of the plan to provoke a war in the following spring: so long as the provocation looked plausible, French support was apparently assured, and Garibaldi himself was cast for command of the volunteers. At once he became an enthusiastic and wholehearted supporter of the government.

Soon afterwards he had his first meeting with the King and was greatly impressed. He hoped that Victor Emanuel would command the army in person and disregard current criticisms that the sovereign was completely incompetent as a soldier. Garibaldi wanted an unlimited military dictatorship to be proclaimed, so as to put an end to chatter and the squabbles of politicians and parliament; and the King should be that dictator. "The national will has already chosen the King as our supreme *duce*". Naturally enough, however, the politicians at Turin saw things differently, for this extension of royal power could be only at the expense of parliament.

Garibaldi's desire for a royal dictatorship was one sign of the undercurrent of differences which continued between Cavour and himself. Cavour genuinely wanted the friendship of the radical democrats, as they would strengthen his forces and their manifest support would lessen the danger of Mazzinian revolution. But he did not particularly like or trust the King, and equally he did not want Garibaldi inflated too much. When it came to the point, the numbers of the volunteers were kept down; Garibaldi was not to command all of them; the best applicants were drafted instead into the regulars; and the rest were left with old-type muskets and neither artillery nor engineers. Cavour agreed with General Lamarmora, the minister of war, that volunteer units were politically dangerous and militarily undependable; and the regular soldiers were especially anxious that the irregulars should not emerge from the war with too great a lustre.

Count Cavour was an aristocrat and a diplomat, and did not fully trust or understand the popular forces that were working alongside him in the Italian *risorgimento*. When Mercantini wrote his famous hymn for Garibaldi's volunteers, Cavour in January 1859 called it ridiculous because there were already too many national hymns. He was usually too much a realist to appreciate ideal motives, too pragmatic to like strong popular enthusiasms, too conservative and exalted to be unpatronizing or quite at home with the masses.

In March 1859, just before Cavour arranged to provoke the "unprovoked aggression" by the Austrians which justified his war of liberation, Garibaldi was made a major-general in the Piedmontese army and given the volunteer brigade of *cacciatori delle Alpi*. The red shirt was forbidden; the men had blue trousers and grey coats; Garibaldi put on a general's finery and trimmed his beard to accord with regulations. Only his inevitable American saddle and the off-white poncho and red neckerchief softened the effect of this novel and uncharacteristic gold-braided uniform.

The volunteers were the usual mixed assortment of idealists and charlatans, chivalrous enthusiasts fighting alongside the outcasts of society. Many of them were students; some were just out for excitement, romance, and heroism; the great majority could now properly be called Garibaldians, enthusiastic votaries of a new and growing cult.

Only a few days were allowed for training and creation of an *esprit de corps*, but Garibaldi defied orthodoxy and declared that a fortnight was long enough to make a soldier. He alone knew the proper admixture of ingredients in this particular recipe. While the regulars had the advantage of good discipline and training, Garibaldi knew far better than they the value of enthusiasm and how to instill it. Although soldiering was his profession, he was anything but a professional soldier, and passionately he extolled unpaid volunteer action in the service of an ideal by people who knew what they fought for and loved what they knew.

In his own original way he was a born commander. His practical and far-from-textbook training had given him an intuitive sense of tactics and fitted him to evaluate military situations with extraordinary speed. He could adapt a plan in a moment, and, right or wrong, it would be applied with the greatest resolution. All planning and organization were kept as simple as possible to allow for speed and flexibility; and this was precisely where the Piedmontese army proved least effective by comparison. He knew how to fight for the initiative, how to keep up the pressure, and how to win the legendary reputation that accompanies continual success. Never did he let himself be rattled. Above all, he really was fearless— caring nothing, it seemed, for death, and acting as if he were invulnerable.

Self-confidence of this sort was infectious and won him the absolute confidence of his men, as he already had their love and admiration as an ideal figure of legend. He may have had few ideas of his own, but Guerzoni well points out how wrong were the people who thought him just a pawn in the hands of others. Invariably his force of character imposed itself on everyone in his immediate presence. He kept his own counsel, and rarely let second thoughts or other opinions disturb a plan of action. Francesco Crispi, the future prime minister and great friend of Garibaldi's, said that he had never known anyone with a stronger will-power. This testimony, from a person who was himself so inflexible and domineering, carries conviction.

The original idea in forming the volunteers had been that they should fight *alla partigiana*, a partisan war "to disorganize the Austrian army, interrupting communications, blowing up bridges, cutting telegraph lines, and burning stores of food, clothing, and fodder" —so ran Garibaldi's order of March 1 before war began. The primary object was to encourage the people of Lombardy to revolt. "Wherever the revolution is successful, the person who enjoys the greatest esteem and trust among people will assume civil and military power". He should try and win over the people by abolishing the taxes on food. He ought to take ten conscripts out of every thousand inhabitants and commandeer horses, money, food, and so forth, always issuing receipts. Martial law should be imposed and no newspapers allowed, and deserters should be executed inexorably.

This first scheme was later abandoned, partly because Garibaldi's idea of a popular, insurrectionary war caused alarm in Turin, partly because facts did not bear out the widespread assumption that Italians everywhere were yearning to fight for their freedom. Many Lombards were, willingly or unwillingly, in the Austrian army itself, and Garibaldi recognized that these included some of the best elements of the province. Nor did the Austrians ever lack Italians in the Lombard villages who would spy for them on Garibaldi's military movements. In any case, most of those who believed in nationalism had repeatedly been instructed to eschew anything so insidious as a Mazzinian insurrection, and had been taught instead to depend on conservative Turin and a Piedmontese initiative. They knew that a popular revolution would be looked at askance by Turin, and, furthermore, to assume the burden of chasing the Austrians out when the Piedmontese army was at hand seemed an unnecessary risk; whereas, in the event of the Austrians winning once again, it would be as well not to be compromised in advance. The tragic failure of 1849 had made Lombardy suspicious of Peidmontese intentions and abilities.

When war began late in April, the volunteers were not after all employed to stir up the plain of Lombardy, but were placed to create a diversion on the extreme left flank, while the main force of about 60,000 Piedmontese and 120,000 French dealt with the Austrian army. Garibaldi did not have a full division, only three half-strength regiments—about 3,500 men in all. He moved quickly, by nocturnal marches as he always preferred, and so secretly that not even his chief of staff knew whither or why. One advantage of such a small and independent unit was that he could safely leave his own lines of communication far behind. He crossed the River Sesia and then the Ticino over a week ahead of the Piedmontese, and volunteers in civilian clothes went still farther ahead to spy out the land. "Anyone who can wield arms and does not fight is a traitor," said his proclamation: "Italy, free from its foreign oppressors, must take the place which Providence has assigned it among the nations."

Although not very much was gained practically by

Garibaldi's diversion, it was finely executed. One or two obvious mistakes are easy to point out afterwards, but with no cavalry or artillery he defeated the Austrians on May 24 in a classic engagement at Varese and so opened the way to Lake Como. Until about June 9 he was cut off from news and supplies. He knew nothing of the Piedmontese and French movements until he read in the newspapers that they had won at Palestro on May 31 and Magenta on June 4. By that time he was over the River Adda. With better equipment and support, or if given all the volunteers—as he had asked and thought he had been promised—he might have done much more, and the legend would not have gained ground that Cavour and Lamarmora were trying to keep him quiet and lessen his influence.

On June 9 Garibaldi was summoned back to Milan by the King. Decorations were handed out, but in a way which caused much discontent among the *cacciatori,* and he himself was not called upon to give advice. Henceforward his unit lost its independence and was merged into the general advance; it was a rôle that he never much appreciated.

The volunteers had done well but not brilliantly. He was much ashamed that in a small engagement at Treponti the regulars had seen his men in a panic retreat, and in his touchy way he blamed the King for purposely depriving him of promised support so as to diminish his prestige. But, as he well knew, sudden panics occurred frequently with these raw militiamen. His own proclamations show him trying to drum *sang-froid* into them and reproving them for frivolous alarms. By letting off guns without even seeing the enemy, they often shot their own friends. Their discipline was bad. They persistently carried too much personal baggage. Too many of them were leaving ranks under pretext of accompanying the wounded.

He even had to chide them once for sack and vandalism. Clearly the *cacciatori* were by no means an ideal fighting-force.

The war shortly came to a premature close. After Magenta the allies lost touch with the enemy and wasted valuable time dawdling while their opponents regrouped. Garibaldi was highly incensed at this over-cautious and desultory advance. He himself was moved back out of the front line. The volunteers had doubled or trebled in number by casual recruitment, and though this may have seemed natural and proper to him, it no doubt aroused political suspicions at headquarters, and must have posed supply problems that he could not appreciate.

On June 24 the two main armies drifted into an encounter that neither had intended, and a terrible but indecisive battle was fought at Solferino. But here Louis Napoleon called off the war as having gone far enough, and the armistice of Villafranca was forced on an unwilling Cavour several weeks later. It was not in the interests of France to create too large and strong a kingdom at her back door, and Napoleon correctly divined that Cavour was intriguing privately to win more from the war than their bond had stipulated.

CHAPTER EIGHT

AGAINST THE GOVERNMENT

1859-1860

THE armistice of July 1859 distressed Cavour because he had reckoned on winning Venice as well as Lombardy and so forming a compact kingdom across the north of Italy. Garibaldi, however, shrewdly saw its advantages. His continual fear had always been that Cavour wanted merely to enlarge Piedmont in the north instead of to create a wholly unified Italy; and if Venice had been captured, northerners might then have rested content with having chased Austria out of the peninsula. The aim of national independence might thus cut across the aim of national unity, the good might be inimical to the best. Garibaldi likewise feared Cavour's alliance with the authoritarian and imperialistic ruler of France. Italians should deliver themselves, or else they might find that a France which had gained for them both Lombardy and Venice might retain and reinforce her protectorate over the north. It was no good turning out Austria just to replace her with another master.

Garibaldi sadly concluded from recent events that Italians were not yet ready or willing to deliver themselves. Almost no southerners at all, he complained, had joined his volunteers. Even in the north he had recruited only the educated, the townsmen, and these were "weakened by an effeminate life and untrained in masculine activities". They had not been tough enough to stand long forced marches, and were always complaining about their food. He compared his countrymen unfavourably with those Spaniards who, against the first Napoleon, had turned every house into a centre of resistance. "The Italians have too much individual egoism and too little love of their country."

During the remainder of July Garibaldi suffered from another attack of rheumatism, and he lived quietly, reading Cæsar's commentaries. But when an invitation arrived from Baron Ricasoli to command the forces of Tuscany, this was too good a chance to miss. It was a great opportunity to keep up the pressure in the centre and south so that the existing configuration

F

of a still divided Italy should have no time to become habitual and accepted.

The war in the north had been the signal for revolutions to break out in the independent duchies of central Italy. Ricasoli at Florence had chased away the Grand Duke and made himself a virtual dictator; Farini had carved out for himself a similar position in the former Duchy of Modena; and Bologna and the northernmost province of the Papal states had also declared their independence of Rome. All these revolutionary governments subsequently clubbed together into a Central League and invited the Piedmontese General Fanti to lead their joint armies. Garibaldi arrived in August as second in command, a little piqued to find himself assigned to play second fiddle when he had hoped to call the tune.

His task was to hold the Papal frontier against a possible counter-revolution, but Fanti also empowered him to march into the Papal states in support of any other town, such as Ancona, that might join the revolution. This was a dangerous order to give to so fervent a nationalist as Garibaldi, and it brought out into the open a major split in politics. The primary concern of Ricasoli and Farini was only to break free from the rest of central Italy and to link up with Piedmont-Lombardy in the north; and they feared that to go any farther in the centre would provoke European feeling to prevent this partial northern union. Garibaldi was useful to them, for his prestige made him a wonderful focus for recruitment of volunteers, and he alone could discipline and train the recruits. But they had intended to employ a subservient instrument, and were alarmed to discover that he might have different political and military views about the expediency of a further nationalist movement over the Papal frontier.

Garibaldi, for his part, soon discovered that they were not confiding in him, and that his independent popularity was resented. Fanti had been appointed over his head, and his own subordinate officers apparently had instructions that he might be disobeyed. Orders were issued and then inexplicably countermanded in an atmosphere of secrecy and subterfuge. It was an ambiguous and embarrassing situation, and highly explosive.

In his *Memoirs* Garibaldi bitterly lamented this missed opportunity to invade the Papal states, and the tortuous intrigues that had frustrated him. The government at Turin, too, had played him false. When he went to see Victor Emanuel he had been given to understand that he could push forward on his own so long as he took full responsibility and was ready to be repudiated if he came to grief. But the reports of the British minister suggest that the King was all the time exploiting Garibaldi in a project to annex Tuscany, by first warning foreign diplomats that the Garibaldians were out to spread the revolution into southern Italy, and then suggesting that they could be controlled only if the Piedmontese were allowed to march into Tuscany and stop them.

Both the King and Ricasoli were thus trying to exploit Garibaldi for purposes of their own, and fully deserved the embarrassment that ensued. To complicate matters, neither Ricasoli nor Farini quite saw eye to eye with each other, and Fanti had a dual allegiance to them and to his King. This helps to explain the double dealing and contradictory orders that made Garibaldi feel so thwarted. Ricasoli did not dare dismiss him, because he had good reason to fear that the government which challenged this popular idol would not survive for twenty-four hours.

Late in October the position was so complicated

that Garibaldi was summoned to see the King at Turin. We can guess what was said, for after his return to Rimini he speeded up preparations for a revolt, and Guerzoni overheard him planning a general invasion. Obviously Victor Emanuel was still playing a double game, using Garibaldi to frighten Europe into allowing a partial annexation, yet letting this unruly subject take all the responsibility and the kicks: the King stood to gain either way, accepting any conquests if the revolution won, or stepping in to restore order if it lost.

For a few days longer the scheme for invasion went on. Arms were smuggled across the frontier, ships were prepared, and small units of men were sent to instigate the insurrection that would give the pretext to invade. Then suddenly Victor Emanuel was frightened by the diplomats into drawing back from this irresponsible venture, and hurriedly sent another of his generals, who halted the revolutionaries just before they crossed the Rubicon. Summoned again to Turin in the middle of November, Garibaldi obeyed and resigned. The King, as usual, was not only doing the deceiving, but subsequently managed to blame the deceit on his ministers and Fanti. He realized the importance of keeping the personal loyalty and affection of this volcanic and dangerous guerrilla, and to do this he was quite ready to play off subordinates against one another. His official government had so far co-operated reasonably well with the revolutionaries, but this deception by the King left everyone openly at odds once more.

On November 19, Garibaldi publicly decried "the miserable foxlike policy that for the moment is holding up the triumphant progress of the Italian movement", and which had tricked him out of his freedom of action as a general of the Central League. But he did not impugn the King, only the ministers. Indeed, he

charged people to rally round the brave and trust-
worthy Victor Emanuel, who would say when the
time was ripe again for revolution. He told Hudson:

"The king has risked his life in the cause of Italy.
I love and respect him. He is a man of his word,
and his political situation is difficult and unfortunate.
He has explained it to me, and as he is of opinion
that my stay in the Romagna may be prejudicial to
the cause of freedom in Italy, I should have been
wanting to myself and to my country had I not
immediately acceded to his wishes."

For the rest of 1859 Garibaldi remained in a highly
excitable condition. Italian nationalism was the "cult
and religion of my entire life". He opened subscriptions
for a million rifles and a million men. In public
speeches he declaimed that "the whole nation must
become an army in itself". The regular soldiers of
Piedmont had proved insufficient, and "because the
ministers distrusted the popular national element in
the country, we therefore had had to fall back on the
shameful expedient of calling in foreign armies to
defend us".

This accusation came too near the truth to be gain-
said. The King reacted by trying to siphon off this
superfluous enthusiasm and asked him to organize the
national guard in Lombardy. But Cavour was furious
at even this small sign of royal complaisance toward a
potential rebel. A dangerous fissure was opening inside
the national movement, splitting the Right from the
Left and the administration from the King.

Garibaldi's frustration was cleverly nourished by
the Left-wing opposition in the Turin parliament, who
tried to make him form a society to rally for the
elections all the small groups opposed to Cavour. At
first the radical leader refused, explaining that he was

no parliamentarian and never liked any political group-
ing which was less than the totality of the nation. Then
he yielded to pressure and founded the short-lived
Nazione armata, and it seems that some of this pressure
came from the King, who secretly harboured several
private grievances against Cavour.

Cavour and Victor Emanuel had engaged in many
sharp words—for instance, over the King's signature of
the armistice, over the marriage of his daughter, and
over the monarch's improper private life. On the other
hand, Garibaldi was someone the King could appreciate, a bluff, frank, soldierly man with a firm sense of
loyalty and without the subtle finesse and secondary
aims of a politician. Garibaldi was always genuine, and
what he said rang true even if it was silly; whereas
Cavour was guileful and dissembling. Moreover, there
was the significant distinction that Cavour used
parliament to control the King, while Garibaldi, on the
contrary, advocated a royal dictatorship to control
parliament. Cavour was too much a civilian for the
King, who liked people in uniform. He was also too
clever: the King had good reason for preferring
character to intelligence.

Hence, at the end of December, Victor Emanuel
summoned Garibaldi once more and, from what could
be discovered by third parties like Massari and
Hudson, he spoke very harshly of his prime minister.
From this moment can be traced that ominous idea in
Garibaldi's mind that he could always rely on the King
against the normal constitutional government of the
country; or, worse still, that the King might not be
sorry if someone were to oppose and overthrow that
constitutional government. The situation has a slight
and superficial resemblance to the attitude of the
King's grandson towards Mussolini just before the
march on Rome in 1922.

A few days afterwards, in January 1860, even Victor Emanuel joined in the gross laughter over a tragic and delicate interlude in Garibaldi's life—his second marriage, to the young Marchesina Giuseppina Raimondi.

This lady was aged seventeen, while he was fifty-two. She had met him in June 1859. He himself has recorded that soon after their meeting he proposed to her on his knees outside a hotel on the lakeside at Como, but she was no more enthusiastic than Speranza had been; and, as he put it, "strong in that *amour propre* and that masculine dignity which has never abandoned me in similar circumstances, I decided to forget her".

Subsequent events are not clear, but he was surprised to receive a more accommodating letter towards the end of the year, perhaps prompted by her father, the Marquis, who was an enthusiastic Garibaldian and espied a good match for his illegitimate daughter. Garibaldi replied, nervously listing various obstacles to their marriage: first, he had just had a daughter by his servant Battistina Ravello; secondly, such a marriage might mean some diminution in his popularity, which would be a national loss in the event of a future war; then his age, his failing health, his poverty, and his "natural melancholy", which would not suit her high spirits. But she answered that all this had been taken into account.

At the end of 1859 Garibaldi was out riding with Giuseppina when a restive horse ran away with him for several miles and crushed his right knee against some masonry. As a result, he had to spend three weeks in bed at her father's house. This clinched the matter, and on January 24, 1860, they were married in the family chapel. Immediately after the service a letter was placed in his hands and he was seen to

become furious. Confronting her with the letter and
hearing her admit its imputation, he even raised his
hand in anger. She was heard to say that she had
thought to marry a hero and here he was only another
brutal soldier. Suffice it that he went off and never
saw her again. Many explanations have been given
of this dramatic and unedifying scene. Almost certainly
she was going to have a child by one of his officers.
But the extraordinary timing of the letter indicates
that there must also have been some sort of calculated
plot. His own sentiments were that someone was
making a public fool of him, and that was one thing he
would never forgive.

Garibaldi was as headstrong in love as in battle.
He was far from irreproachable in his relations with
women. Unorthodox about marriage, he eventually
married his third wife only because of their children.
"I cannot understand people dying for love of a lady,"
he wrote among his rather humourless and insipid
epigrams, "when the world is so full of others." Three
different women were possible wives for him in 1859,
and it was tragic that he chose as he did. But this
mysterious affair cannot have been the shattering blow
to him that some have said. The whole episode had
been a little forced, and an hour or so afterwards he
was again deep in political correspondence.

Meanwhile, his slight attempt to rally the parliamentary opposition had come to nothing, for the
various factions could not agree; and, likewise, his
interlinked campaign for general military training and
the *Nazione armata* simultaneously collapsed. People
apparently would not join his new society. The diplomats at Turin, headed by Hudson, were apprehensive
over its provocative name, and they acted to prevent
"that well-meaning goose" from covertly enlisting his
old volunteers in a mobilized national guard for dark

purposes of his own. Yet another explanation of the failure of the "armed nation" comes from Guerzoni, who concluded that Italians were not a military nation with a latent military spirit as Garibaldi seemed to think; nor was the prevalent social system such as would allow the existence of anything like the German *Landwehr* or the English Rifle Volunteers. This conclusion came from an officer in the volunteers who had himself been wounded in the campaign of 1859.

Garibaldi could not agree with such a defeatist argument, but he always obeyed Victor Emanuel, and, at the request of the *Re galantuomo*, he dissolved the *Nazione armata*. At the same time he publicly apostrophized the king "to give us not liberties but battles". Everyone was invited instead to subscribe to his fund for a million rifles, and indeed the King, as well as Mazzini, contributed. Garibaldi himself subscribed five thousand lire, but later confessed that he had paid only a thousand and left the rest until a future date when he might possibly be in pocket. The government allowed this fund to exist, for it might one day be useful in time of war; moreover, Garibaldi had shrewdly put two of Cavour's supporters in charge of it; and also the rifles were carefully kept under lock and key in government depots. But not even such an unofficial venture to encourage a wider Italian policy was very popular at Turin. Most of the contributions came from elsewhere than Piedmont, and only a few thousand of the intended million rifles could ever be bought with the sum realized.

In January 1860 Garibaldi was still not fixed in the rigid opposition to Cavour and the liberal-conservatives in parliament which was to make the rest of this year so difficult. He wrote to a friend that Cavour might do much good if only he would prove that he sincerely wanted an Italian nation and was not just a Pied-

G

montese at heart. Even Cavour's evident distrust of
the volunteers in the war of 1859 could be forgiven
if he would rely on the Italian people rather than on
the manœuvrings of diplomacy. What finally divided
these two men was Cavour's politic decision that, if
they wanted French support for further moves in
Italy, they must sacrifice to Louis Napoleon the frontier
province of Savoy and Garibaldi's birthplace, Nice.
Both districts were therefore signed away in a secret
agreement of March 1860.

As an elected deputy for Nice, Garibaldi stormed
into parliament for one of his rare appearances in that
unfriendly atmosphere of Turin. Disregarding all
parliamentary forms, just as at Rome in 1849, he tried
to insist that the matter be raised at once, but was
compelled to wait a week. He then spoke to urge that
this cession of national territory was unconstitutional
because Cavour had signed the agreement without a
word to anyone and without the slightest discussion
in parliament. The alienation of an inherent part of
Italy proved that the idea of a nation meant nothing
to the prime minister. He was trafficking in peoples
in a manner that "was now repugnant to the general
conviction of civilized men". It was also a dangerous
precedent, and might shake peoples faith in the future
of Italy: for Cavour might as easily alienate Sardinia
or Naples in the interests of an enlarged Piedmont.

What chiefly annoyed Garibaldi was that the loss
of Nice made him "a foreigner in his own country".
Nice was Italian, and Cavour had once said as much,
though now he was asserting the contrary. "I know
something of history too," said Garibaldi, "even though
people may say that I am better able to fight than to
argue before so many honourable and learned men."
At least he knew that the plebiscite held at Nice was
a fraud, because with threats, bribes, and police action

any popular vote might be conditioned. Cavour was using sham democratic forms and terminology to conceal the hollowness of his pretensions to liberalism.

All Garibaldi could do in practice, however, was to resign from parliament in protest against "this illegal and fraudulent agreement". A certain English adventurer tried to persuade him to make a commando incursion into Nice on plebiscite day to overturn the voting urns; but in fact he did no more than tentatively ask the United States minister if he would use his American influence to make Nice an independent state.

When his temper subsided, Garibaldi had been turned wholly against Cavour. No matter that the cession of Savoy and Nice purchased the connivance of France in Piedmontese annexation of Tuscany and the central duchies. It was wrong in itself, it was a crime of *lèse-nationalité*. Cavour was enslaving Italy to French patronage—to the France, moreover, of the same tyrant, Louis Napoleon, who had crushed the Roman republic of 1849.

Garibaldi was equally disgusted with parliament. He saw it as a corrupt, cowardly body, in which gerrymandering, intrigue, and the hope of private gain made deputies into rubber stamps for the all-powerful minister. Parliamentarianism at Turin was merely another fraud, where the use of "influence" by the government had time and again bought retrospective indemnity for breaches of the constitution. People now noted that Garibaldi was speaking in the "language of a Cromwell". It was a dangerous sign, especially as even Cavour had to recognize that his opponent was "one of the greatest forces in Italy"; and it meant that the various ideas on how to constitute a nation might soon be in open conflict.

CHAPTER NINE

SICILY CAPTURED

1860

A KINGDOM of northern Italy was now virtually in being which included Piedmont, Sardinia, Liguria, Lombardy, Tuscany, the central duchies, and a small part of the Papal states. The main areas still outside this union were Naples, Sicily, Rome, and Venice, without which the kingdom could hardly be considered a proper nation. It was in the year 1860 that Garibaldi's conquest of the south altered the whole picture and brought into being an all-Italian state with a more Mediterranean character and a Mediterranean destiny. Judged purely by practical results, it was the greatest achievement of his life. Very few people even in Italy can have envisaged this as a possible and desirable outcome of events, but his single-minded determination brought about an astonishing triumph over men and circumstances.

By the beginning of 1860 he was a professional nationalist obsessed with the thought of unifying his country. In January 1860 he had stated that if the south was ready to revolt, they could count on his aid, though first he wanted proof of readiness. Too many earlier patriots—notably Bentivegna, Pisacane, and the two Bandieras—had perished because they had set out to deliver Naples and Sicily and then found southerners uninterested. Although impetuous in action, Garibaldi was cautious before action began, and seldom inclined to initiate anything on his own. If he hesitated now, it was not from any democratic conviction about first consulting southern opinion, for he had just told the U.S. Minister, Daniel, that "liberty itself must sometimes be forced on the people for their future good"; it was rather because of a prudent unwillingness to take unnecessary risks.

Mazzini's friends did their best to make him take the risk, and meanwhile stirred up revolution in Sicily to convince him that it was feasible. Loath to commit himself beyond recall, however, he waited four weeks more to see if this revolt developed successfully, and in the meantime assembled men and munitions at Genoa.

Unfortunately, the guns purchased with the Million Rifles Fund were sequestrated by the government, and Cavour refused to authorize their release. Colonel Colt sent a hundred of the revolvers that had proved so wonderfully effective a weapon in Texas, and some new rifled firearms arrived from the Royal Ordnance Factory in England. What was more important, the Ansaldo armament firm surreptitiously underwrote Garibaldi's expedition and positively incited him to action. A thousand muskets were also produced by the National Society, but these were smooth-bore converted flintlocks that had been superannuated from the regular army. They were rusty, and nine-tenths of them, said Garibaldi, would not fire, but this dictated a tactic of bayonet charges which he knew well how to use.

Money came in by driblets from many sources, among others from Lady Byron and the Duke of Wellington, and the newspapers were full of subscription lists from Italians at home and abroad. The towns of Parma and Pavia gave especially large sums. Nevertheless, private contributions were difficult to organize, and under one pretext or another many debts had to be contracted which could never be repaid.

Volunteers meantime gathered at Genoa. One
observer noted that nearly half of them were less than
twenty years old. Many were students hoping to avoid
their examinations and trusting that a grateful country
could not subsequently be so churlish as to refuse
them their degrees. Of the 1,089 people making up
the "Thousand" who landed in Sicily, Bergamo provided 163 and Genoa 154, while at the other extreme
Rome provided 11, and Turin only 7. Young Menotti
Garibaldi was with them. There were refugees hoping
to return to Sicily, poets out for romance, unemployed
with nothing to do, a number of common wastrels and
roughnecks, but the majority were patriotic idealists.
The youngest was eleven, the oldest had fought under
the first Napoleon. A dozen were one day to become
generals in the regular Italian army, and Crispi and
Cairoli were future prime ministers. There was even
one woman, Crispi's mistress.

This was Garibaldi's greatest venture, yet it barely
succeeded by the closest of margins. Even among his
political friends many tried to hold him back from
such a madcap enterprise, and at the end of April he
nearly went away home to Caprera. Cavour not only
gave no encouragement, but used his influence to try
to stop the undertaking, and then attempted to have
another leader appointed in whom he could place more
confidence. Cavour would even have liked to use
force to arrest the thousand if only he had felt stronger
and Garibaldi were not riding on a crest of widespread
popularity.

In the end, the hotheads—Crispi and Bixio—pre-
vailed. After a sudden decision the latter seized two
paddle steamers of about two hundred tons each and
came to collect Garibaldi at Quarto on May 6. There
were many last-minute hitches. Bixio was six hours
late, and all night long the others were painfully riding

ROCHESTER INSTITUTE OF TECHNOLOGY LIBRARY

out a big sea in small boats. At the last minute there
was no ammunition, for some of the stores had been
stolen during embarkation. Nevertheless, Garibaldi had
no hesitation in ordering that the expedition should
go forward. The time for caution was over, and he was
not a person to have any more second thoughts.

No one knew quite who had managed to get on
board. Garibaldi put on his general's uniform to review
them before he changed into his normal costume of
red shirt, grey trousers, white poncho, black felt hat,
and the silk neckerchief of South American days. Some
of the others had military or naval uniforms, but most
were in civilian clothes, a motley gathering that did
not lack even clerical garb and the frock coat of the
man about town. Such a miscellany was not easily
turned into a cohesive, disciplined force. On the
crowded decks, officers were hastily chosen, and Garibaldi's staff worked out a provisional organization while
he himself wrote a war song and tried to set it to
various tunes by Verdi.

Twice they stopped en route to Sicily—once to
steal some coal, once to persuade the colonel in charge
at Talomone to imperil his career by giving them
munitions. The die-hard republicans left them here,
for Garibaldi had firmly decided on the programme of
"Italy and Victor Emanuel". Later on he blamed himself for not having had the courage to declare himself
candidly a republican; but in 1860 he was more of a
realist than many supposed or than he subsequently
recollected, and his decision to support the King was
natural and politic. At that time neither he nor most
of his men cared very much about internal politics so
long as Italy were made.

At Talomone he also sent sixty volunteers off on a
diversion to deceive people by a mock invasion of the
Papal states. This was not a clever move, and it accom-

plished little except to make Cavour belatedly try to stop the expedition at all costs. There was a French garrison in Rome, and Cavour could not afford to endanger the alliance with France upon which he based his whole policy.

Not even Garibaldi knew their precise destination until the steamers were just off Sicily. It depended on whether and where the revolution was still alive. His two boats had once lost contact, and their search for each other luckily caused some delay so that they missed the Neopolitan warships trying to intercept them. Off Marsala a boatload of fishermen was captured to provide pilots, and in two hours the ships were empty, just as the Neapolitan navy came within shooting-range. The Garibaldians seized the Marsala telegraph office and sent off false messages, while Garibaldi at the town hall roundly declaimed that all who did not fight on his side must be either traitors or cowards.

The local inhabitants were not quite sure whether he was a deliverer or just another of the countless invaders who had bedevilled their unfortunate country. He proclaimed himself a dictator in the name of Victor Emanuel, the "constitutional King of Italy", and under these dictatorial powers he requisitioned blankets, food, and what cash he could find in each township. Equally unpopular, and no doubt less effective, was his edict conscripting all Sicilians between the ages of seventeen and fifty.

But while in some villages the local inhabitants ran away as he arrived, elsewhere they began to join him as few people ever had in the north. For he took the taxes off salt and *pasta*, and promised to divide up the large estates and distribute the land. Sicilians in the expedition were deliberately sent to stir up a peasants' revolt in the interior, and soon in the eyes of the masses he was becoming a fabulous figure of heroic proportions. Unexpected allies were found in some of the poorer clergy, who were themselves an oppressed class and made excellent propagandists among the common people. One of them, the Franciscan Fra Pantaleo, attached himself as chaplain to the Thousand.

The Bourbon King of Naples had twenty thousand soldiers to defend Palermo, and first a small unit of three thousand was sent out under General Landi to crush this petty and not very promising invasion. The two forces met at Calatafimi, near the famous Greek temple of Segesta. Landi was in a strong position, but Garibaldi was determined to risk all on a single throw. Whether or not the Sicilians followed him would depend on how quickly he proved to be the invincible *duce* that rumour maintained.

It was a straggling, undisciplined battle. The few guns that would fire began to open up despite Garibaldi's express orders, and then there followed a disorganized charge that his bugle calls could neither stop nor direct. Up the steep slope they went with desperate fierceness, taking seven separate terraces at the bayonet's point. It was a victory for sheer courage, as tactics scarcely entered into the battle and Garibaldi had little hold on events. But it does not seem to have occurred to him that he might lose; and this was proof that such an unreasonable and fortuitous sort of bravura paid off in practical terms. "Here we either make Italy or we die," he is reported to have said. The result, at all events, was conclusive, first in opening the way to Palermo and, second, in convincing the Sicilian irregulars watching on a near-by hill that Garibaldi was a man who won.

A general exhortation was now issued for everyone to take a scythe, an axe, even a nail on a stick, and pick off the Bourbonist sentries, cutting communications and ceaselessly harassing the enemy. There is no doubt that in countless unspectacular and often unrecorded ways this was done, and it was the decisive stroke of victory. Fires on every hill meantime spread the news of insurrection. To impress his audience, the sceptic Garibaldi also attended Mass and received a crusader's cross at the altar. This would help to win local confidence, and, anyhow, he was too mystical a character not to find some significance in such a ceremony.

For three days his men had to live in the open under torrential rain. Dressed in their requisitioned clothes, they appeared a regiment of friars, for religious houses were the best if not always the most willing source of supplies. They marched all night along difficult hill paths, thus concealing their movements and keeping the enemy always surprised. Once as a tactical deceit they were ordered to retreat at the double, but this was nearly disastrous for the morale of the Sicilian irregulars. The only hope was to go forward and take Palermo somehow or other, and so demonstrate that nothing could stop them. The fate of the whole expedition hung upon another miracle.

Garibaldi had little more than three thousand poorly armed irregulars with which to attack a large fortified town. But he had prestige, and he had the desperate courage of a man risking his life for the thing he most valued. During these few decisive days he also had the very important help of a peasants' revolt that terrorized the police and soldiers and brought local government to a standstill. From inside Palermo, representatives of a revolutionary committee managed to reach his camp in the guise of American officers and give him plans of the garrison. Co-ordination was nevertheless almost impossible. Everything had to be improvised, and his men were not the sort that responded easily to orders and discipline.

Fortune favoured the brave. By skilful diversions and clever use of mock campfires in the surrounding hills he caught the Bourbonists off their guard. When he attacked, some of them were thus out on a wild-goose chase. The remainder were not ready nor had they been trained for street fighting, and after a few hours of confusion Garibaldi found himself in posses-sion of most of the city. The first signs of success had gradually induced the population to join in with a will, to build barricades, and to work off the old grudge of Sicilians against Neapolitans, poor against rich, governed against governors.

General Lanza now was compelled to ask "His Excellency, General Garibaldi" for armistice talks aboard a British man-of-war. The latter held out for better terms than he was offered, and by absurd bravado won his point. The Bourbon garrison astonish-ingly capitulated on condition that they were allowed to sail home to Naples. The unbelievable had hap-pened, and this preposterous filibustering raid had been justified by success. For the following six weeks Garibaldi was able to take stock of his good fortune and prepare the next step.

The government of Turin was no less delighted than amazed that he had won a new province of Italy without provoking the diplomatic intervention they had feared. Cavour therefore quickly dispatched a commissioner to annex the island to Piedmont, and at last provided direct help in money and munitions. On June 10, Medici sailed in reinforcement with three thousand more volunteers in the *Franklin* and *Washington*.

Garibaldi, however, while glad of these much-needed reinforcements, meant to keep hold of his revo-

lution as long as possible. With some justice he feared
that, if Sicily was under a Piedmontese commissioner,
perhaps the government would not allow his revolution
to proceed further. He himself firmly intended to go
on as far and as fast as possible while the going was
good: probably to Naples, if possible to Rome, perhaps
even to Venice. This would constitute an open challenge to France which Cavour would be obliged to
prevent as soon as Piedmont had completed the annexation of Sicily. Garibaldi therefore, while restating
his firm allegiance to his sovereign, decided to hold
on to his autonomy until he could proclaim Victor
Emanuel king of a united peninsula. The Turin government could always disown him if his efforts miscarried.

This was to be Garibaldi's first and only experience
of governing. As dictator of Palermo he inhabited a
small suite of three rooms in the royal palace. By now
he was a tremendous hero to the Sicilians, especially
because he was so evidently a dedicated person without any aristocratic airs or northern disdain. Projects
of governmental reform were adumbrated. He set up
a school under one of his officers in which the street
urchins of the town could receive the rudiments of
military and other instruction, and he himself frequently came and gave them short lessons in patriotism and morals. He made a good-will tour of the local
convents—occasionally the nuns sentimentally kissed
him in turn, even the mother superior, and almost
every day they sent him presents of sweets and
embroideries.

Despite his views on religion, Garibaldi was
realistic enough to celebrate the local feast day of
Santa Rosalia by visiting her grotto in pilgrimage. At
pontifical Mass in the Cathedral he even sat on the
royal throne in his red shirt, claiming the apostolic
legateship traditionally held by the rulers of Sicily.

This notorious unbeliever there stood as defender of the faith, with his sword bared as the gospel was read. Small wonder if the common people ascribed to him the magical powers of someone directly in communion with God.

Success had multiplied the number of the volunteers. Apart from Sicilians, there was a foreign contingent composed largely of Hungarians and French, and every few weeks other expeditions arrived by sea from the north. A foreign newspaper correspondent estimated that there were soon ten thousand first-rate troops, every day better disciplined and inured to fighting, able to march a daily thirty miles on little food. Such a scratch army was bound to contain some unworthy elements, but the Englishman Commander Forbes thought it much above the average: "For sobriety and good conduct generally, this undisciplined force far surpassed any regular troops." Garibaldi was ruthless in shooting people for even stealing grapes, just as easily as he shot them for desertion in face of the enemy.

Even in matters of dress they continued to be of all varieties, because some officers would not permit the red shirt, sensibly maintaining that it was a good target and betrayed their numbers. The eccentric Countess della Torre had arrived, booted and spurred, with a white braided hussar tunic, to which she added a Spanish plumed hat and a sword that clanked in an alarming way as she walked. There was plenty of comic opera here, and Dumas, for one, revelled in and contributed to it. His luxurious yacht, well stocked with champagne and accompanied by another exotic lady who sported an admiral's uniform, was given over by day to making red shirts, as he excitedly watched events on behalf of a Paris newspaper.

In the early stages Garibaldi had profited greatly

from the aid of the Sicilian peasants, who had risen
in a primitive and often horrible vendetta against the
landed proprietors and the Bourbon government. Later
in the summer, however, as their life reverted naturally to its normal prosaic and pedestrian course, these
same peasants sadly and hopelessly divined that Garibaldi was not, after all, a social reformer with a magic
solution to their eternal starvation and distress. On
the contrary, at the Nelson estates in Bronte we even
find him having to put down a "communistic" movement that impeded military progress. The peasants
were not strictly interested in this political war, only
in a social war of their own which cut right across
politics; but so violent and unruly were they in seizing
land and cattle that the landowners, even those who
were politically most reactionary, were forced to see
that the only hope of law and order lay in protection
by this radical dictator and his revolution. Here was a
tremendous, if accidental, gain to the cause of unified
Italy, because the landowners were the most solid and
coherent class in politics. Their gradual and often
reluctant transference of allegiance to the insurrection
was a decisive event in Italian history and helped to
make possible the next phase of this astonishing
conquest.

The surrender of Palermo had allowed Garibaldi
to occupy almost all of Sicily except Messina and its
environs in the north-eastern corner, but he needed
another victory to consolidate his gains and assure a
safe passage to the continent. On July 20 he made
contact once more with the enemy. Discovering that
they expected reinforcements, he made a quick attack
on the fortress town of Milazzo against better-armed
troops who knew the ground. The battle went to and
fro for eight hours, and the Garibaldians had their
worst casualties yet—eight hundred killed and

wounded, four times as many as their opponents. It was a heavy price to pay for their legend of invincibility, yet they trusted their leader absolutely, and in return he led them to success. Dumas came ashore afterwards and found his hero sleeping from exhaustion on the bare stone floor of a church with his American saddle as a pillow.

Messina itself was too strong a garrison town and had to be bypassed. The more immediate problem was how to transfer more than ten thousand troops across the straits under the guns of hostile forts and navy. Some people thought that they would make a beachhead at Salerno, forgetting that almost no ships were available. The cabinet at Turin tried to stop them from crossing at all, fearing an involvement with France and the approach of revolution up the peninsula; but the King privately encouraged them to chance their luck and prepare to be repudiated if events went awry. It was a muddled and ticklish moment, and only Garibaldi was quite sure of himself.

CHAPTER TEN

DICTATOR OF NAPLES

1860

THE conquest of Sicily still left half the population of geographical Italy outside the Italian nation that was rapidly taking form and consistency; and the Straits of Messina were the first impediment to any further advance. Without adequate transport, let alone a navy, Garibaldi's way was barred by the Neapolitan fleet, which was larger even than the Piedmontese. In addition to his ten to fifteen thousand men, the radical leader Bertani had collected another eight thousand in the north for a pincer movement down through the Papal states. This joint force was more than Garibaldi had ever commanded before, and supplies and organization were becoming a real problem. As always, he had no foreordained idea in his mind, but let circumstances dictate his strategy, ready to seize the moment with energy and skill. Meanwhile, he kept his own counsel, leaving his officers and men to trust blindly in his judgement and fortune.

On July 30, once the Battle of Milazzo had brought him within striking-distance, he ordered Bertani to begin the attack that ever since May they had been preparing on the northern frontier of the Papal states. This forced the Turin government at last to declare its hand openly, because such a movement threatened an immediate clash with the French troops in Rome. Cavour abruptly put a veto on any further recruitment of volunteers, and compelled Bertani to take his private army off to the politically less dangerous area of Sicily. Garibaldi came to meet Bertani in Sardinia, but was too late to divert this separate expedition and make a second front. The whole episode is an example of the serious difficulties of co-ordination which confronted him now that the chessboard was becoming more intricate and involved.

Back at the Straits of Messina, he pushed ahead with his plan for a general landing in Calabria aimed at Reggio. He had already sent over a Calabrian named Musolino, who was trying without success to sow dissension among the Bourbon garrisons there. It was important to keep the enemy guessing. As Cavour was at last showing these novel signs of active hostility, speed was essential; the momentum had to be kept up, and, if anything, they had to gather impetus. To deceive the opposing navy, several boats were sent westward right around the island, and as they came up again to Taormina a small mobile force quickly and quietly boarded them on August 18. The thirty-mile crossing was made by night, and was not intercepted.

There were about 16,000 soldiers holding Calabria, and against this number Garibaldi's advance unit was composed of only 3,500 men. He marched fearlessly on Reggio, bombarded it from the hills, and forced the surrender of the garrison two days after his landing. The main body of Garibaldians then crossed over and began their triumphant march up the toe of Italy.

The general panic was such that their opponents never had time to recuperate or regroup. Garibaldi could even leave his men behind and travel ahead almost alone, trusting in the fabulous reputation now attached to his name. The enemy rank and file threw away their arms, and sometimes savagely killed their officers. By the end of August, ten thousand had surrendered.

This was an unchecked course of three hundred miles in the summer heat, with fever common, amid great difficulties over commissariat. But Garibaldi had discovered that Cavour was plotting a rival *coup* of his own at Naples, directed as much against the revolution as against the Bourbons, and there was thus need for hurry if he wanted to make Naples a base for a further march on Rome. With unlimited courage and uncommon military intuition, Garibaldi went ahead full tilt.

Around Salerno there were reputed to be 40,000 Bourbon soldiers and Garibaldi was ready for a pitched battle, but he was moving too fast and the morale of his opponents was negligible. Even the Neapolitan ministers and generals had begun to change sides and

H

accept bribes from Cavour. On September 7, Garibaldi
and half a dozen companions entered Naples, covering
the last stretch from Salerno on the first line of railway to have been built in Italy. He had quite out-
stripped his army, and the Bourbon soldiers were still
in the fortresses of the city, but instead of firing on
him, they presented arms as Garibaldi stood up in an
open carriage on the way to his hotel. Perhaps this was
the finest hour of his life, and the citizens cheered him
to the echo when he addressed them in the piazza from
his balcony.

Naples was the largest town in Italy, capital city
of its largest region and, indeed, the third-largest town
in Europe. Garibaldi ruled it as dictator for two months
while he prepared for the last decisive battle against
King Francesco, who had retreated along the road to
Rome.

Only a few dozen Neapolitans seem to have joined
Garibaldi's now very sizable army, yet perhaps it is
not so paradoxical that the city gave him the biggest
ovation he had ever received and the reception committee was quite swept away in the general surge.
At such moments he showed at his best. He took care
to pay his early respects at the shrine of their patron,
Saint Januarius, and shortly had the satisfaction of
knowing that the blood of the saint had miraculously
liquefied in approval of his victory. On the first evening there was cheering until late in the night; finally
one redshirt came out and mimed Garibaldi asleep,
whereupon a sudden silence fell and everyone tiptoed
home. On the second night he attended the opera at
the San Carlo Theatre; in reply to the cheers, he called
out from his box: "*Viva Vittorio Emanuele!*" and the
whole audience took up the cry from him. It was all
good fun, good theatre, and good politics.

Garibaldi's short dictatorship was a complete

novelty for Naples, a highly coloured and almost dreamlike parenthesis in its history. His bold legislation took little root and did not survive his departure. He brought in tentative schemes of social reform, free education, and railway construction, and even tried to abolish gambling, though human nature and a dead weight of history and geography were all against him. What he had seen in the deep south made him aghast at the results of clerical privilege and monopolies. He therefore allowed Protestants at last to build churches, and hard on his heels came an influx of Diodati Bibles. He also dissolved the Jesuit houses and nationalized their property, and when the Archbishop refused to sing a Te Deum in endorsement of the saint's palpable benediction, the offending prelate was bundled off into exile.

In politics the dictator attempted the praiseworthy but difficult task of preserving a nice balance of forces between Left and Right. The radical Bertani was appointed his secretary, but his ministers were chosen from moderate conservatives close to Cavour. For a few days he went on assuming that both radicals and conservatives could now agree on at least the national question. He had good grounds for believing that Victor Emanuel would support the revolution while it continued successful, and the prodigious events in Sicily and Naples seemed to make a further attempt on Rome at least a fair gamble.

Militarily, a march into the Papal states was a legitimate speculation, and if as many Neapolitans as Sicilians had joined Garibaldi's forces, it might have been as difficult for the Bourbon army to dig in at Capua as in Calabria. Politically, it was, to say the least, risky to challenge the whole might of Catholicism at its nodal point, especially when French soldiers garrisoned part of the city of Rome itself. But there

was a widespread expectation that the Pope was about
to leave the Vatican and that the hour for ending his
temporal power had come. This expectation existed
not only at Naples, but also at Rome and in governmental circles at Turin. The English minister at Naples
thought that Garibaldi's idea of advancing farther was
stark madness, "but one must admit that his landing
at Marsala did not appear a much less desperate undertaking". Certainly it was only Garibaldi's absurd over-
confidence that had allowed him so far to win half the
peninsula for a new Italian state.

Garibaldi was so convinced of this, and so trusting
in Victor Emanuel, that his first action in Naples was
to turn over the Neapolitan navy to Piedmont. These
were the ships that he would have needed for the
amphibious operation on Rome he now had in mind.
He must have believed that Cavour could not stand
out any longer against the torrent of national feeling,
and he did not guess that the prime minister now had
another contradictory and equally bold plan of his own
to capture the movement that had been quite long
enough under the auspices of the radical Left. Later
on Garibaldi condemned himself for thus losing the
initiative, and admitted that he must have been too
busy fighting to concentrate properly on politics.

Most of the leading Italian radicals were now in
Naples. The Milanese Cattaneo was there, who wanted
a federal republic, and Mazzini himself arrived from
England but was not allowed any active part in affairs.
Crispi and Bertani were still there hoping to use Naples
as a springboard for further revolution. They could
not persuade themselves that Cavour was even yet a
convinced nationalist, because his opposition to the
sailing of the Thousand, and to their crossing the straits,
and to their capture of Naples, all betokened a defeatist and untrustworthy attitude. It seemed to them

that the events of 1860 had so far put Garibaldi in the right and Cavour in the wrong, by justifying a popular national movement which owed nothing to diplomacy and governmental bargainings with the foreigner; and this popular movement ought to continue.

It was unfortunate that the King had his own reasons for playing off Garibaldi against Cavour and so increasing these divisions. He was always restive under constitutional trammels, and for most of this year he had been going behind the backs of his own ministers and encouraging Garibaldi to defy them. If Garibaldi won, the King stood to gain enormously in power and territory; if he lost, then the Crown could always refuse to take responsibility: and Garibaldi understood and even welcomed this equivocal situation. Earlier in the year Victor Emanuel had even reached the point of telling one of his generals that he would rather have Garibaldi than Cavour as prime minister. Now in September he sent a private royal message straight to Naples, and the dictator responded first by publicly demanding Cavour's resignation and then by proceeding towards an attack on the Papal states. There was reason to believe that these were the royal wishes.

Cavour, however, now that this rift could no longer be concealed, threatened to resign and expose the King's double-dealing and leave him to face the responsibility. Victor Emanuel was in this way forced to give up his dual and ambiguous policy; confronted with a choice, he sensibly decided to fall in with the more moderate policy of his ministers which had such overwhelming parliamentary support.

The dramatic way in which Cavour at long last recaptured the initiative from the revolutionaries was by Piedmont invading the Papal provinces of Umbria and the Marches from the north. Louis Napoleon was

cleverly persuaded to allow this by being told that the
invasion was really intended to check Garibaldi's
further advance. It was a daring and conclusive move.
It bypassed Rome, leaving the Pope untouched and so
satisfying France, and at the same time it captured
most of what remained of the Papal states and the
whole of southern Italy which Garibaldi had already
conquered. By a single stroke this put an end to the
revolution and the danger that radical pressure might
be brought to bear on Turin. Only by making it seem
an anti-revolutionary act did Cavour reconcile not
only Napoleon but also the Piedmontese conservatives
to this novel and dramatic union of north and south.

As matters turned out, Garibaldi had been brought
to a halt before the arrival of the Piedmontese, for
when he tried to push on beyond Naples he found forty
thousand of the enemy firmly grouped behind the
River Volturno. In the middle of September the
volunteers received their first and only reverse of
the year at Caiazzo, in Garibaldi's temporary absence.
He had been forced to leave the line in order to com-
pose political differences that Cavour's followers were
creating in Sicily. One of his generals unwisely tried
to force a salient over the river and lost 250 men in the
attempt, not having Garibaldi's gifts as leader and
tactician.

The Volturno valley was notorious for its deadly
fevers. The Garibaldians had few tents, and were not
prepared for autumn damp and the cold nights of
approaching winter. The hospitals, such as they were,
were crowded with cases of malaria and rheumatism.
Now that the period of fast-moving victories was over,
morale was cracking, for this more static type of warfare did not suit them, and they had no artillery to
bombard fortresses like Capua and Gaeta. In any case,
a volunteer army always tended to disband as the

campaigning season ended. They were tired of a life of hardship and glory, especially now that the hardship was more and the glory less. Moreover, the Piedmontese army was known to be approaching to pull any remaining chestnuts out of the fire.

Nevertheless, under these adverse conditions Garibaldi won a great and complicated victory on the Volturno in early October. He had far more troops under his command than ever again in his life, well over thirty thousand in all. It was also novel for him in being a defensive battle, and not the quick and simple type of skirmish at which he was so adept. On the contrary, with inferior numbers he had to hold a long line of some twenty kilometres against an enemy determined to recapture Naples before the Piedmontese arrived. Fighting lasted for most of two days. There were over three hundred dead on each side, but the Garibaldians held firm and took over two thousand prisoners.

Many people had assumed that Garibaldi was unable to take on a pitched battle of this magnitude, that he was just a guerilla who could not adapt his tactics to regular warfare. Here the sceptics were confounded by this tremendously important victory. Naples was saved. The politicians and official historiographers at Turin played down Garibaldi's achievement for political reasons, and exaggerated by contrast the modest victory of the Piedmontese over a greatly inferior force of Papalists at Castelfidardo. The King was intending to take over government from Garibaldi, so it was important that his prestige should be built up and Garibaldi's reduced, and a great deal of effort was addressed to both these tasks, with only partial success.

For the rest of October Garibaldi had to remain on the defensive. He expressed himself as delighted that the King was coming with the northern army to conquer part of the Papal domains. Although he strongly suspected the political intentions of the Turin government, he luckily did not know that Cavour was giving orders that the Garibaldians should, if necessary, be attacked and thrown into the sea. Nor were such orders justified, for he had more sense than Cavour ever allowed, and civil war was far from his mind. When the northern generals and officials arrived, he acknowledged defeat gracefully and did his best to make their task easy, though it was notorious that Cavour had carefully selected as governors of Naples and Sicily the half-dozen or so people who for personal and political reasons were most sharply antagonistic to the radical leader.

Early in November Garibaldi formally surrendered his conquests, after a plebiscite had declared by a huge majority for a united Italy under Victor Emanuel as constitutional sovereign. Most of Garibaldi's laws and reforms were now rescinded, his public-works contracts countermanded, his appointments quashed—Dumas, for example, lost his much-prized superintendence of the excavations at Pompeii. Whether or not because he was jealous of Garibaldi's great popularity, the King failed to appear at the farewell dress parade of the volunteers which had been put on to greet him. Victor Emanuel took an instant dislike to his new subjects, and preferred to dally with his mistress and go off hunting every day rather than condescend to the tiresome duty of greeting the expectant crowds.

There were discourtesies on all sides. The King appointed Garibaldi a full general and offered him lands and possessions, but the latter crumpled up the notice of his appointment, saying that he was not to be bought off with material rewards. The revolution would be needed again one day, and he must keep his independence and his reputation intact and clear from all official taint.

When Garibaldi departed in the *Washington* on November 9, the official Press was deliberately mute. He sailed at dawn so that there should be no demonstrations, but at least the foreign ships in the bay saluted his departure. It was a fine and dignified withdrawal, for, despite numerous slights, he was determined to make no difficulties and no fuss. He was vastly relieved to be free again from all the business and rancour of public life. With a few provisions and some seed for his garden, he returned to the obscurity and poverty and loneliness of Caprera.

CHAPTER ELEVEN

POLITICS IN THE NEW ITALY

1861-1862

To ease his departure from Naples, Garibaldi had been given to believe by the King that he would be needed again when the next campaign weather came round in four months' time. He assured his volunteers, as he assured the British admiral when he went to say good-bye, that by next March they would be in the field with the whole nation in arms. At Naples he had also given a farewell interview to Mazzini in which these two revolutionaries discussed how it might be possible to oust Cavour during the winter and start another war against Austria for Venice.

With this remotely in mind, the Dictator of the

Two Sicilies returned for the interim to what he pleased
to call the "vineyards" and "fields" on the barren rock
of Caprera. It was remarked that he looked as happy
as a schoolboy home for the holidays. At once on landing he set loose his two battle horses. His general's
uniform was given to one of his labourers, and an
English lady later found the man digging potatoes in
this strange costume and bought it.

Caprera was soon made by his presence into something like a tourist attraction, and the mail packet-boat
arrived at Maddalena each Friday with visitors. Some
people wanted autographs, some wanted jobs; secret
envoys from Mazzini and from the King travelled
thither, Russian socialists, fans, cranks and enthusiasts
of every description. It seemed as though the bother
and the intrigues of public life were doing their best
to pursue him. But he tried not to let them interfere
with his work on the farm, and people who came to
waste his time often received short shrift. Growing
food for his household was the first call on his time,
and he also had the far-fetched idea of making his
children's fortune by the sale of granite.

Like Cavour, Garibaldi found his great relaxation
and inspiration in agriculture, and in census returns
he described himself simply as "farmer". He would
regularly be found hoeing (there was little purchase
for a spade in the shallow patches of soil), or breaking
up granite and making walls against predatory wild
goats. Visitors were amused to note that he called his
donkeys after Pius IX, Franz Joseph, and Louis
Napoleon, but his horses after Marsala and Calatafimi.
A more than ordinarily useful visitor in 1861 was a
professional English gardener called Robert Webster,
who was sent out by well-wishers to help him.
Garibaldi usually kept an account book to show his
purchases and sales. In its pages we see him pruning,

grafting, manuring, trying to control his shepherds, importing olive plants, and sowing his lucerne only when the moon was old. There was also wildfowl to shoot, and his friends have left accounts of expeditions every two or three days on which he speared fish from a rowing boat. It was a tranquil and happy, if not materially prosperous, existence.

The early 1860s were the years of Garibaldi's greatest vogue and notoriety. The U.S. minister, Marsh, wrote home to his government in 1861 that, "though but a solitary and private individual, he is at this moment, in and of himself, one of the great Powers of the world". His fantastic victories, followed by his almost equally fantastic abdication into humble private life, made him talked of as a character out of Plutarch. The man who had been absolute governor over half of Italy often possessed not even a single change of clothing, and did not scruple to wash his own shirt. His friends even used him as a tailor, for he had learned in his travels to cut and fit by eye and was always handy with a needle. Humility and pride can sometimes go together, and in Garibaldi the amalgam rang true. This was the secret of what Commander Forbes called his "irresistible spell", for, unlike Victor Emanuel or Cavour, he was patently an honest and genuine man without concealed aims. Hence his ability to conjure up a makeshift army in no time out of nothing, and then to dispense with routine discipline; he had in him naturally that which was obeyed.

Often, no doubt, there was something about this admiration which would make any true liberal highly suspicious and distrustful. Mazzini, torn between disapproval and jealousy, commented that it was politically alarming and morally unworthy for Italians to throw themselves at a dictator's feet; but the same Mazzini was also envious when seventeen thousand

people in Brighton each contributed a penny towards
a gift for his ex-pupil. The excesses of admiration were
sometimes even morbid. Cavour, with sly humour,
on one occasion sent several authenticated locks of the
hero's hair to London for select distribution to the
faithful, and a possibly apocryphal story relates how
Garibaldi himself once had to tell Lady Shaftesbury
that his hair was growing again and he would send
some more when he could spare it. One newspaper
account describes a senior officer standing guard over
him and combing down his hair after each visitor had
taken her toll. It was a nasty form of hero-worship
when high-toned foreign ladies intrusively waylaid
him for a kiss and sought out his room to collect nail-
parings and the hairs from his comb; and such adula-
tion may well have gone as dangerously to his head
as did the secret incitement to revolutionary action
which continually arrived from the King.

The trouble was that Garibaldi now knew himself
to be a power in the land. A celebrated future foreign
minister of Italy, who had served with him as one of
the volunteer *cacciatori*, noted that he already was
regarded by the populace almost as the head of a new
religion. In Lombardy the women had held up their
children for him to bless. In the south he had commanded an army of nearly forty thousand, had been
treated as a demigod by peasants and the Neapolitan
mob, and had felt them throb to his flamboyant
speeches. Not only had he put himself on a level with
Cavour and the politicians, but several times he had
thwarted their policy and dictated their conduct. He
thrilled to feel himself a kingmaker who had already
done more than anyone else to reconstruct Italy, and
he felt sure that it was his destiny to round off the
kingdom by conquering Rome and Venice.

It was disagreeable for the administration at Turin

in 1861 to have such a man in possession of a grievance, an open rebel against the whole system of
government. Cavour and parliament had arrested his
revolution, so he retorted in public that the deputies
were cowardly and the ministers too little convinced
of Italian nationality. In his memoirs he baldly asserted
that there was far too much corruption about Italian
parliamentarianism for it to be a healthy influence in
public life. Subsequently this view became a dangerous
commonplace among both progressives and conservatives; but for the moment it was a heresy, and even
more dangerous and offensive.

Just as Cavour knew how to manage parliament,
and felt himself strongest when parliament was sitting,
so Garibaldi understood the people and felt strongest
when the populace was replying in chorus to his
flourishes and rhetorical questions. "There is a sort of
intimate communion of mind between Garibaldi and
the masses which is positively electrifying," said a war
correspondent in Sicily; and the rhetoric that might
sound bombastic to sedate visitors from elsewhere was
evidently well attuned to the fervid imagination of the
south. Garibaldi had without doubt succeeded in capturing the imagination of southerners, and in retrospect
his short dictatorship, with little enough reason, took
on the proportions of a golden age. Parliamentary
government after 1861 was by comparison prosaic and
flat, and the subsequent failure of parliament ever to
settle the south thus helped to generate a real collision
of principle and practice.

It was not a simple conflict between a constitutional
Cavour and a dictatorial Garibaldi. The differences
between them were more subtle and shaded, and
Garibaldi was even able to appear before parliament
and bluntly accuse Cavour of violating the constitution. Although Cavour believed fervently in parlia-

mentary forms, his enemies argued that this was only because a submissive parliament was so easily manipulated into making him a virtual dictator. Garibaldi, on the other hand, though dictatorial by temperament, had neither the ambition nor the intelligence to play the Mussolini.

Not being in any sense a clever person, Garibaldi was certainly muddled in his political views. He was coming to conclude that in order to make Italy a great power, in order to make Italians put aside their differences and live in mutual tolerance, nothing less than violence and coercion would suffice. But this was far from being a positive disbelief in liberty. Paradoxically, strong government was needed to establish freedom and tolerance. In England, which remained his model state, genuine liberty might possibly exist without excessive government interference—and so much the better. But in Italy he feared that Cavour meant to set up a type of pseudo-constitutional government like that of Louis Napoleon, under whom liberty was a hollow sham.

At the beginning of 1861, general elections were held for the first parliament of the new kingdom of Italy, and Cavour obtained a great majority. Garibaldi at first refused to stand anywhere, as he felt convinced that cleverer and subtler men would always win where it was a question of manipulating elections and assemblies. But the swiftly multiplying grievances of the south finally persuaded him to accept nomination at Naples, and he was elected there almost without opposition.

His programme was concord and national unity, and he even tried to compel the government to allow Mazzini to return from exile. So long as the ministers were prepared to accept revolutionary nationalism, he was behind them. "I do not greatly care whether

Cavour or someone else is prime minister," he said, "so long as half a million soldiers are ready to fight by next spring." Cavour, however, being entangled in diplomacy, could have no further truck with this dangerous form of popular national war, and preferred to rely on French diplomatic support. So Garibaldi drifted into opposition. He felt sure that Louis Napoleon would not be anxious to have a unified and anti-Papal Italy on his southern frontier.

The real clash came over Cavour's disbandment of the Garibaldian soldiers left behind at Naples. Instead of being treated with honour, these volunteers were considered a political embarrassment, especially as the regular army was jealous of their success and their easier discipline and promotion. Many of them had given up their families and livelihood for the national cause, yet they were being treated with greater severity than the Bourbon soldiers whom they had defeated. These guerrillas might have been extremely useful to Italy in the protracted civil war that now broke out in the south against the King's government; instead, they were hurried off to their homes, or else left to emigrate and fight in the American civil war.

On April 18, 1861, Garibaldi overcame a very painful bout of rheumatism sufficiently to go and raise the whole question of his volunteer army in parliament. He entered among the befrocked deputies in the most unparliamentary costume of red shirt and white cloak, carrying a Spanish sombrero. As Guerzoni commented, this love of strutting in strange costumes somehow fitted his independence and originality of character; but to his auditors on this occasion it seemed grotesque and calculatedly provocative. Luckily for Cavour, the staid and frowsty atmosphere of the Turin parliament told heavily in favour of conservatism. The ministers had begun to suspect again that the King was abetting this potential rebel, and that a *coup d'état* was on the cards.

On this occasion General Fanti first made a long and dull speech trying to justify his treatment of the volunteers. Then there was an angry and tactless reply by Garibaldi which even accused Cavour of provoking civil war in the south. The prime minister was pale with fury as he asked for protection against such an insult, and the atmosphere at once became charged and electric. After the session had been suspended in disorder, Garibaldi apologized and hoped that Cavour would change his mind and keep the volunteers in being. But the latter refused to compromise. He recognized that it was a crucial point, not only between two policies, but between contradictory theories of government, and he felt strong enough in parliament to be inflexible. Garibaldi declared himself utterly unsatisfied, and was cheered from the galleries. Nevertheless, the voting went against him, 194 to 79.

As a sequel, General Cialdini published an extraordinary statement roundly abusing everything from Garibaldi's politics to his behaviour and costume. This seemed like deliberate provocation to a duel, but fortunately Garibaldi had too much sense and too much good-humour. He simply and quietly replied that he had a perfect right to speak his mind in parliament, and that he would choose his own clothes until he heard that it was no longer a free country. At the King's urgent wish, he then had a meeting with Cavour, and the official newspapers inaccurately let it be known that the two were reconciled. Cavour had refused to yield an inch. The prime minister was by now a sick man, weighed down by all the problems of reconstruction, and several weeks after this imbroglio he suddenly and tragically died. A severe fever so baffled the doctors that they could only bleed him "until no more blood would come".

The calamitous death of Count Cavour left no one else in Italian politics who had half so clear a head or so skilful a technique, for his colleagues were mediocre men and he had kept all the strings of policy in his own hand. With such men in power, evidently no further move towards Rome or Venice would be possible for some time, so Garibaldi retired again to Caprera.

Abraham Lincoln then offered him command of an army corps to fight for the northern states in America, and Garibaldi went so far as to ask and receive the King's permission to accept. Garibaldi addressed Lincoln with unaffected admiration: "America, who instructed our fathers in liberty, is once again opening a solemn hour of human progress, and makes us sadly wonder why old Europe cannot find the intellect or the heart which can rival her." Again, he told the German Karl Blind that "America should increase in power so that it might act as a check and counterpoise to the aristocratic and tyrannic Powers of Europe". But arrogantly he replied that he would go and fight for Lincoln only if two conditions were satisfied: that he was made supreme commander, and that slavery was formally abolished. He had been let down before by politicians and superior officers, and was not anxious to expose himself again to a situation in which he would not be his own master. There the matter was dropped, though Garibaldi again offered his services the following year when the federal army had less need of them.

Abolition of slavery was one of those humanitarian projects very dear to such a radical reformer. He had proudly released slaves wherever he found them in South America. Italians, too, he insisted, must stop

I

bowing and scraping to authority, or they would be hunchbacks for ever. "Man is born free, and must fix his eyes boldly on heaven itself."

The early 'sixties found Garibaldi associated with a number of such generalized projects for emancipation and reform. For instance, he successfully appealed to the King for the reprieve of certain people condemned to capital punishment, and in 1862 signed a petition to abolish the death penalty altogether. Continuously through the next twenty years he encouraged the growth of mutual-help societies among the workers, as he believed that "the future greatness of Italy lies in particular with the working-classes". It was a prime duty of the wealthy to improve the condition of the poor so that the dangerous gulf between riches and poverty might be lessened. Here he proved to be more sensible than the general run of his own and subsequent generations; this political *ingénu* instinctively put his finger on perhaps the chief cause of governmental instability and internal strife down to our own day.

Another field to which he progressively turned his reforming zeal was religion, as he gradually matured his particular brand of heterodoxy. It was sacrilege to believe in the religion of Rome and what he named the "satanic race of priests" who were vowed to keep Rome isolated and Italy divided. The true religion was that of Christ—the religion of humanity, as he came more commonly to call it—based on the equality of all men and the priesthood of all believers.

By 1861 he was also framing his utopian belief in a frontierless community of nations where all men would belong to one family and wars would be impossible. He addressed a candid memorandum to the Great Powers about creating a European federal union and stimulating a general "regeneration of politics such as the genius of the century demands". In the new world here envisaged, "the immense capital sums now being diverted from the real needs of the poor to human destruction would instead be spent on a colossal development of industry, on improving roads and bridges and canals, and on building schools to educate and improve the lot of those now destitute".

These doctrines of universal peace and brotherhood were all a little oracular and indeterminate, however much they showed that his heart was sound. In practice he was a nationalist, even a bellicose nationalist, convinced that it was perfectly right and proper for the peace of Europe to suffer so that Italy could be made. He reconciled these irreconcilables in a further extravaganza. Nations should all help each other secure a rightful place in the sun, and then wars and despotisms would cease for all time on this earth.

CHAPTER TWELVE

SARNICO AND ASPROMONTE

1862

RADICALS and conservatives alike in Italy were chafing for the acquisition of Venice and Rome whether by fair means or foul, and slowly by their importunity were forcing Europe to concede this as inevitable. In April 1861, replying to a communication from no less a person than the British foreign minister, Garibaldi wrote to say that, much as he hated war, armed conflict alone could finish off the process of unification, and that he hoped victory was only a few months away. The whole of Europe seemed ripe for a nationalist explosion against the outmoded composite empires of Austria and France, and he was as firmly convinced as was Mazzini that Italy had a divinely ordained mission to ignite the detonating spark.

Had these radical revolutionaries only known it, Cavour himself in his last months of life was smuggling large consignments of arms into the Balkans for use in some future war against Austria, and was indignantly protesting his innocence and blaming the radicals when the British caught him at it. Cavour was utterly disinclined to promote a revolutionary war in Italy, but was a real Garibaldian when it came to setting fire to houses other than his own.

The government was more rash and less calculating than people said; on the other hand, so was Garibaldi more circumspect and politic than his general reputation allowed. The United States minister now wrote as much to Secretary of State Seward, confirming that Garibaldi showed consummate prudence and would gamble only on good chances. The statement of policy issued from Caprera in June 1861 laid down that the revolutionaries ought to take up any enterprise that promised probable success, but the success must look probable, and that meantime they had better all wait until public opinion tired of the ineptitude and indecision of orthodox politicians.

For the rest of the year he was all bark but no bite. When sympathizers in Melbourne sent him another sword of honour, he took occasion to rail against the cowards and incompetents who would not move on towards a unified nation. Rumours circulated that he meant to go and capture Fiume in the Adriatic—one thinks of 1919 and D'Annunzio. He was visited in Caprera by the German socialist Lassalle, who was trying to enlist him in a project of general European revolution. All the time he kept quiet and said nothing, while volunteer organizations went on collecting arms and subscriptions for the day when his flag would again be raised.

In December 1861 Garibaldi paid a quick visit to Turin, and in government circles it was noted with alarm that he had come for a private audience with the King. Early in 1862 the prime minister, Ricasoli, no doubt under pressure from the Court, sent Senator Plezza under cover of a hunting-expedition to Caprera with a message that the government would once more like to co-operate with him. Soon afterwards, however, Victor Emanuel abruptly dismissed the intractable Ricasoli for being insufficiently deferential to the Throne. The next premier, Urbano Rattazzi, was a subtle courtier, far less scrupulous and more accommodating. Garibaldi again left his island, this time ostensibly to carry out an official campaign for the encouragement of rifle practice among the people. He had an express invitation from the government, and one may be sure that he would not have moved from home without the expectation of some further enterprise of pith and moment.

On arrival in Turin he saw both minister and King, and seemed fully satisfied with what they privately told him. Then at Genoa, without any government opposition, he presided over a congress representing all the democratic nationalist groups in Italy. Mazzini alone was not present except in spirit, but wrote to draw Palmerston's attention to this imposing assembly of the flower of Italian patriotism. There is little doubt that the government had undertaken to give Garibaldi one million lire for an expedition against Austria in the Balkans. Perhaps they intended by this to keep him occupied well away from Italy; perhaps it was part of a concerted move on Venice; we do not know. Anyway, full of confidence once again, Garibaldi proceeded on a clamorous progress through Lombardy, brazenly summoning university students and even schoolboys to practice fighting in the intervals of their work, and everywhere teaching his technique of popular insurrection.

The two tragic misunderstandings of 1862, at Sarnico and Aspromonte, have still not been completely explained. Was Garibaldi acting for the government directly? Or was he acting indirectly, to be owned or disowned according to his measure of success? Or was he acting for himself alone?

On any interpretation, Rattazzi was playing a disingenuous and provocative game. Garibaldi's campaign tour was at the government's invitation and at government expense. He started out with deputies and ministers coming and going around him, living in a senator's house, asked to dinner by princes of the blood royal. At Milan his host was no less a person than the provincial governor—who noted carefully that he was cheered resoundingly in the streets but received hardly a clap from the *beau monde* at the opera. At Cremona he even called on the bishop. Wherever he went, he was officially banqueted by mayors and prefects who made florid patriotic orations. It went to his head, all this fiery atmosphere, and gave him the illusion that he had his finger on the national pulse, when really all the speeches and applause about Venice and Rome were but sound and fury signifying nothing at all. Perhaps Rattazzi had not considered the effect of this popular hysteria on such a volcanic temperament. At all events, Garibaldi was not the man to be satisfied with speechifying and vocal acclamation, and the government discovered that they had given him a blank cheque which he could present for payment when and where and how he chose.

At the end of April he arrived at Trescorre for a three-week stay, ostensibly to take the waters for his infirmity, and there his supporters assembled. He was visited by an aide of the King's. Messages were sent to Turin for the money promised, and an attempt was made to raise loans in England; meanwhile, agents perambulated the cities of northern Italy gathering clothes and subscriptions.

At a secret meeting he took the very unusual step of consulting with his lieutenants. He put to them a considered project for taking Venice by means of a landing in Dalmatia, and assured them of government collusion if they were successful. It was a stormy meeting, for some of the caucus feared the strings attached to this equivocal sort of government aid, and suspected a plot to lure Garibaldi out of Italy to his destruction. The general belief, and it was not implausible, held that the government had arranged with France to sacrifice him on a diversionary expedition while Louis Napoleon simultaneously began the war the French had been preparing on the Rhine. Jessie White says that the majority was against him, fearing some dubious involvement with imperialistic France, and preferring to wait until a movement inside Venice showed that people were ready for a popular and less Napoleonic and more "Garibaldian" war of liberation.

To the world at large, however, and to Rattazzi, this meeting had seemed like a dangerous assemblage of enthusiastic and unquestioning Garibaldians. No doubt the government had hoped that he would work less ostentatiously and not make official complicity quite so obvious. They now became alarmed. In the middle of May, therefore, Garibaldi's house was suddenly surrounded and Colonel Nullo and a hundred volunteers were arrested at Sarnico. Whether France had called off her war, whether Rattazzi saw that he was playing with fire, whether several departments of state had been working at variance unknown to one another—whatever the explanation, it was a dismal misunderstanding and the result was bloodshed. Rattazzi, when taxed in public, ambiguously stated that the million lire had been meant simply to encourage emigration. In private, to the British minster he admitted that he had been trying to push these volunteers into the Balkans, but had then discovered they aimed at a move on Venice. It was an embarrassing and incriminating confession.

Garibaldi was furious, for a good hope was lost, and having given people to expect government connivance, he was now discredited with his own party. Speaking over the dead at Como, he had the crowd weeping and shouting for Venice and Rome; and he himself, clutching and unclutching his cap, was quite overcome and could not continue. In a letter to parliament—he was either too angry or too much afraid to come in person—he passionately contended that the government had deliberately called him out of retirement in Caprera to prepare the next move in national unification, and that Rattazzi had then faltered and arrested these volunteers on the false assumption that they were about to invade the Tyrol. True or false, the government first used all its influence to avoid a parliamentary inquiry into what had happened, and then unobtrusively dropped the prosecution and released its prisoners; but the old breach between Left and Right had been opened wide once more.

Garibaldi's friends thought that he should now break openly with Rattazzi and force the King to define unequivocally how far the radicals still kept any freedom of action. Instead, there were more interviews and private assurances, and he went quietly back to Caprera with all the material for another and bigger misunderstanding. The government had been shaken by this affair at Sarnico, and felt too weak and in too false a position to be properly firm with him.

At the end of June Garibaldi suddenly left Caprera for Sicily. "I am going towards the unknown," he pronounced in his best D'Annunzian vein. In fact, although he said he had as yet no aggressive intentions, he was about to revive the dangerous practice of marching on Rome; and again arises the difficult question of the extent to which he had official encouragement.

Sir James Hudson, for one, thought that Rattazzi deliberately sent him to Sicily, once again as a stepping-stone to the Balkans and as partial reparation for what had just happened in Lombardy. A great friend of Garibaldi's was now appointed governor of Sicily. The Garibaldian committees were in no lack of funds, and one observer noted that all the red flannel on the market was bought up. A strong force of troops existed in Sicily which, if ordered to stop his next move, could have done so without difficulty. But Garibaldi was not stopped. Frequently he referred to having the King's private support, and official denials were never such as would prevent people assuming that he had royal warrant for seeming to take up arms against the King's government.

On the boat that took him and his entourage to Sicily, no one except Garibaldi knew where they were going, nor why, perhaps because premature disclosures had led to the tragedy of Sarnico. Guerzoni, who was with them, later argued that Garibaldi's only motive at first was to use his popularity with the Sicilians to calm their indignation against the government of the new Italy; that, in particular, he was aiming to allay their regrets for the Bourbons and their desire for insular autonomy. On this hypothesis, his project to advance on Rome would have been a result and not a cause of his visit to Sicily. More likely, however, a number of not very clear ideas were simultaneously grinding through his mind.

Each day after his arrival in Palermo witnessed another round of speeches and proclamations. The Sicilians were thrilled at the return of their hero and deliverer, and looked back nostalgically to the glamorous days of 1860. He told the university students that he was tired of the idleness in which he was kept. From the balcony of the town hall on June 30 he positively asserted that Rome would soon become Italian, and in the Garibaldi Theatre on July 2 the people raised a great shout for Rome and Venice, at which he seemed to take fire and redouble the violence of his language. He reminded people that the plebiscites which had constituted Italy in 1860 had voted for a united kingdom—that is to say, they had been a conditional vote, and sovereignty would revert to the people if the government did not soon win Venice and Rome. Here was a theoretical justification for rebellion.

From Palermo he went on a tour of his old battlefields, flowers being everywhere thrown in his path by a delirious throng. At Trapani he forbade the crowd to draw his carriage, for this was degrading to a free people; but he did not protest when at Marsala the cry went up: "Rome or death!" Instead, he caught up the phrase from the crowd and shouted back: "Rome or death!" Again and again they summoned him on to the balcony. Growing more and more excited, he called Louis Napoleon a thief and usurper who worked only for the interests of his family. "Away with the wretch!" he cried, and the crowd repeated: "Away, away!" "Rome is ours!" was his next cry, and they replied in kind.

On the following day, Fra Pantaleo celebrated

Mass in the cathedral, and there was a packed house. The sermon was on Rome and Venice. Summoned by the preacher, Garibaldi lifted his hand towards the altar and took the oath: "Rome or death"; and, from the mayor and corporation downward, the phrase re-echoed through the church.

Back in Palermo after this excursion, Garibaldi took no more advice, nor did his entourage often dare to proffer any. His reception made him think that the whole island was ready to burst into flames. The revolution was on. In no time he had three thousand volunteers, many of them in rags and calling to him for bread, the rest mostly young, ardent, and unreflecting, but all of them caught up by the magic of his personality into thinking that they were on the side of both the angels and the big battalions.

At these signs of open rebellion, Rattazzi again acted as a man embarrassed and uncertain. He dismissed the governor. Proclamations against the volunteers were issued, but were soon torn down: for many of the civic officials imagined that the rebels were working secretly for the King. Perhaps Rattazzi feared as much himself; why else were his orders so vague and hesitant? And why were the soldiers not used to halt the march of this warlike private army? One alternative explanation sometimes given is that most government officials were away on summer vacation! At all events, the volunteers had almost free passage through the island. Anyone barring their path was shown a mysterious document with a big red seal from a metal box, and they were then allowed to pass.

At Catania the regular soldiers took to their heels without a blow and shut themselves up in the castle, leaving Garibaldi for three days virtually governor of the city while further supplies were collected. Foreign consuls reported that he had plenty of ready money. The expedition was not against the King, he was careful to explain, only against the King's ministers, who were deceiving and compromising their sovereign and provoking civil war in Italy so as to gain the goodwill of Louis Napoleon.

Despite the fact that there were naval vessels commanding Catania harbour, Garibaldi was able to seize two merchant ships, embark several thousand men, and cross the straits without obstruction. The order sent from Turin to the navy ran: "Do anything the occasion warrants, but always keep in mind the good of your King and country." The only conclusion to be drawn is that the ministry was purposely vague while waiting to see whether Garibaldi were successful. When subsequently he failed, these naval captains had to take the blame and accept dismissal for their failure to interpret aright this oracular instruction.

Rattazzi's attitude was complex and ambivalent. He was clearly reluctant to use force against such a popular character—especially in Sicily, where autonomist sentiments and a general resentment against the north were running so deep and strong. Once again he fell back on the desperate hope of offering the chief rebel another free passage to America. Meanwhile, his main concern was to use what was happening as a lever on France, by suggesting that revolution in the south could be stopped only if the King's government were allowed to move into Rome. This was to attempt Cavour's policy without Cavour's genius. The present prime minister merely compromised the government without winning his point; while his predecessor in similar circumstances had won his point and not even been compromised.

The King, too, was involved, and his intrigues not only were exposed but also rebounded on his own

head. He privately admitted that the Garibaldians had
been carrying out orders "to a certain extent". They
had now gone much too far for him, but could hardly
be stopped without provoking a major revolution, so
perhaps had better be allowed to chance their hand.
He stood to gain from their success, and perhaps he
could manage not to lose too much from their defeat.
Both the King and Rattazzi were thus victims of their
own bad faith and mismanagement and their misplaced
trust in France. Louis Napoleon could never quite
make up his mind whether or not to withdraw his
troops from Rome and be rid of the thankless task of
defending the Pope. While he still vacillated, it was
difficult for Turin to make any decision.

Once the volunteers were in Calabria, however,
French Catholic opinion obstreperously made itself
felt, and the Emperor decided that there must be no
more shilly-shallying. Rattazzi himself became frightened as Garibaldi approached Naples, for the whole
south was already seething with rebellion, and here
was a new complication to a local civil war that for
some months already had held down ninety thousand
troops in the ex-Bourbon kingdom. During the previous
year martial law had been declared; the Press was
being heavily censored, and stringent measures were
being taken to control what seemed to be a counter-
revolution by southerners against this new government
of the north. Meantime, the regular army in Naples—
and none more than General Cialdini—had been waiting a long time for a chance to measure themselves
against Garibaldi, and a flying column was now
ordered to overtake him and give battle. The intended
victim as yet knew nothing of this. His men lacked
food, and in the drenching rain were having to eat
raw potatoes stolen from the fields. The local shepherds
shunned them as bandits, which indeed in a sense they

were. Unused to long marches, they were footsore and tired, and, without knowing it, were walking in a circle. This was blamed on the deceit of their guides, but more likely Garibaldi was losing his touch. Thus the regular troops were enabled to overtake them.

On August 29, what Cialdini in his report extravagantly called "a fierce combat" took place at Aspromonte. It lasted a bare ten minutes. The ragged army of volunteers did not expect to be fired on by their fellow countrymen and had orders not to shoot, although those commanded by Menotti were unable to stand still without replying. Seven soldiers and five volunteers were killed. Deliberate aim must have been taken at Garibaldi personally, for he was hit twice. Wounded badly in the ankle, he sat down, lit a cigar, and calmly told them to amputate at once if necessary. A curt summons was issued for his surrender, and at this he took offence. Extraordinarily enough, he still could not see himself as a rebel, but quite genuinely imagined that he was an independent commander or world citizen, someone who had renounced all normal state obligations and who should be negotiated with and treated honourably. Cialdini, however, had other ideas.

It was a difficult fifteen-hour scramble down the mountainside to the strait where Scylla looks out upon Charybdis. All night long, with but a short rest in a herdsman's shack, the wounded prisoner was jolted agonizingly. Arrived at the coast, he defiantly asked to be put on an English ship, but his captor had him hoisted aboard an Italian gunboat "like an ox". Garibaldi saluted Cialdini as he passed by, but the latter did not deign a reply. Here was a traitor who had been imperilling the very structure of the state.

The hero had fallen from grace. Some of his companions who had deserted from the army to join him

were now shot out of hand without trial, Cialdini purposely forgetting how desertion had been almost encouraged in similar circumstances before. On the other
hand, the victorious troops at this petty and one-sided
engagement were rewarded with seventy-six medals
for valour, and, besides many other promotions, the
colonel in charge was made a general. The rest of Italy
was not quite so proud of it. Royal proclamations were
torn down, there was hooting and hissing, and at
Messina, for instance, the people refused to let the
band play in the public gardens. It was an exasperated
but ineffective surge of opinion.

As for Garibaldi, he had obtained neither Rome nor
death. His trust in the King had been shaken: surely
it had not been necessary to open fire and then to
execute some of the men who had volunteered to serve
their country. But the government was far more embarrassed. They had to explain why he had not been
halted in Sicily. They also had to decide what to do
with their prisoner.

The cabinet first wanted him tried at law in order
to allay accusations of ministerial complicity; but to
this it was objected that trial by jury might result in
acquittal unless it took place in anti-Garibaldian Turin.
Rattazzi suggested holding a military tribunal, but
was worried that this might alienate popular support
from the administration. The whole question was suddenly dropped when a mysterious "piece of paper" was
brought up at a cabinet meeting, and no doubt this
means that the King's undoubted collusion would have
been bound to receive unwelcome publicity from a
public trial. So this rebel and traitor was set free un-
condemned—even, indeed, with a cachet of popular
approval, and thus felt encouraged to repeat his rebellion at some favourable moment in the future. Neither
public opinion nor important people in governmental

circles took into account how bad this might be for
the country's political education.

Garibaldi had received a compound fracture of his
right ankle. One immediate question was whether he
would die. His passage by boat to Genoa had been one
long torment, especially as there were no proper
medical remedies on board, and his foot became so
swollen that for many weeks no one could be sure
whether the bullet was still in the wound. On several
occasions amputation was again considered. Such
world-wide interest had been created that twenty-
three surgeons came from far and wide to examine
him, before a French doctor at last found the bullet
and it was extracted after eighty-seven days.

Garibaldi's well-wishers in England paid a
thousand guineas to a Dr. Partridge for two visits to the
patient. Lord Palmerston, the prime minister, contributed to this sum, and Lady Palmerston sent an
adjustable invalid bed that proved a godsend. Disgrace-
ful scenes took place at Hyde Park when a hostile Irish
mob ran riot, shouting: "No Garibaldi! The Pope for-
ever!" But, in comfortable Protestant England,
Catholic Irishmen represented a lunatic fringe unworthy of consideration. Cigars and letters poured in
to the injured Garibaldi from all over the world, and
cloth stained with his blood became a treasured relic.
For he was now a public figure—almost, indeed, the
best-known and best-loved figure alive.

CHAPTER THIRTEEN

ENGLAND

1864

GARIBALDI'S wound took years to heal, and pieces
of bone were continually coming out of it. Perhaps he
was never quite the same again either physically or
morally. It was not easy to forget Aspromonte. His
sword was returned to him, and an amnesty bestowed
on all volunteers except those who had deserted from
the army. "You only give an amnesty to people you
consider guilty," commented Garibaldi; but the guilt
lay only in having failed and having compromised the
government; revolution in itself was not wrong, for
here he had had every example and incitation from
the powers that be. Henceforward a new note of petu-
lance crept into his opinions, and the autobiographical
poem that he compiled as a bedridden invalid did not
spare even the King.

The year 1863 he spent being wheeled about
Caprera in an elegant bath chair given by his fans
abroad. His right hand was so crippled by arthritis
that often he could not sign his name. It did not mend
his temper that a subscription which he opened to
help the wounded of Aspromonte evoked only
moderate enthusiasm. Ostentatiously he resigned from
parliament, giving as excuse that it went particularly
against the grain when a harsh rule of martial law was
imposed on the southern provinces for whose annexation he felt responsible. In any case, he was never at
ease in large public conclaves; the only exception to

this was a congress of workers, "because among simple folk I feel really at home".

In great pain on his sickbed, he began to meditate some notable exploit that would wash out the stain on his own and Italy's honour. He wrote of how much he would now like to come and fight for the cause of freedom in America, "of which country I am a citizen", and he appealed to England to help the American north against the slave-owners. If in good health he would almost certainly have gone too to fight for Poland against Russia: Polish emissaries came to Caprera, and some Garibaldians went off to die in Poland.

It is paradoxical to find Garibaldi now writing that there should be no more wars and conquests, and that weapons should be turned into reaping-machines. For at the same time he continued to urge all Italians to sharpen their swords. This was the topsy-turvy logic of his peculiar type of nationalism, which believed in a war to end war. He advocated a generalized nationalism, not just an Italian nation. He would as readily have fought for the independence of Germany as of Italy, he said, and "if Italy ever in her turn threatened the independence of neighbour states, I should regretfully but surely be on the side of the oppressed". Ingenuously but sincerely he imagined that if only all nations were free, then wars would end, and hence several of his lieutenants were now sent out to test the chances of starting a revolution in Transylvania and Galicia.

In 1864 Garibaldi made his fourth visit to England. It was a celebrated occasion, for previously he had been unknown and now he was famous. A musical show on Garibaldi had already run in London, and Garibaldi biscuits and blouses called "Garibaldies" were all the rage. England had perhaps not made many sacrifices for the *risorgimento,* but enthusiasm she gave in abundance, and the enthusiasm was chiefly caused by and focused on this one man. While in Italian governmental circles he was by now highly unpopular, in England he was still the man who had conquered half of Italy for his King.

Newspaper correspondents had therefore chased him; Thackeray had written to ask if he would do a piece for the *Cornhill;* and various committees and organizations had been competing to sponsor a visit by Garibaldi to England. Private individuals came and almost besieged his house. Some of these English visitors wanted just to fête him; some were interested in his views on temperance or workers' education; some wanted to give him good advice and wean him from the party of action. And in particular the Protestants, led by Lord Shaftesbury, looked on him as a heaven-sent weapon against the Pope and an excellent agent for their propaganda.

When Garibaldi suddenly left Caprera for England in March 1864, the news came as a great surprise and shock to Italians. His attack on Cavour, his escapade at Aspromonte, his reprobation of parliament as no place for an honest man were all recent memories, and his great services were either forgotten or else were now being ascribed by official state historiographers to other men. In domestic politics there was only a precarious balance just now. What if Garibaldi were out to collect more money in England for nefarious purposes, and to receive an ovation that might be read as support for the democratic party! He had always been complaining to foreigners that the government was imprisoning his friends and curtailing their freedom of speech. Such accusations abroad would do the administration no good.

His precise motives in going are not easy to fathom. His secretary informs us that few of his decisions were as studied and considered as this, yet he made contradictory pronouncements and appeared not to know himself quite what he hoped to do. Some received the impression that the British government had invited him; others that he wanted to see English methods of agriculture; others that he thought a sea voyage and change of climate would be good for his health.

The most important doubt is whether there was any major political intention. Shaftesbury, who asked him point-blank about this, understood that he had no political object and merely meant to thank Englishmen for their encouragement of Italian nationalism. Guerzoni, however, who escorted him, is positive that many political ideas were running through his mind all the time. Garibaldi used to talk of securing English help for Greece, and for Poland, and for Venice, and of exploiting the Schleswig-Holstein question to mobilize assistance for Denmark against Austria. Palmerston was distinctly worried about possible political designs: he imperatively pressed on all English sponsors "the great importance of making Garibaldi's visit a purely private one, and I urged that he should decline on the score of health all public dinners, at which he would say foolish things and other people mischievous ones".

Garibaldi did make some effort to avoid political demonstrations, but was too big a man to be able to pay a purely private visit. He was now a mixture of hero, saint, national leader, and uncrowned king of the common people. The Peninsular and Orient Steamship Company specially diverted a mail boat to pick him up at Caprera because a director of the company was one of his great admirers. Arriving at Southampton on a rainy Sunday, he found a huge concourse headed by the mayor shouting hurrahs. Garibaldi waved his cap as they docked, and spoke in halting English to say that he had come to thank people for their sympathy.

His first move was to go and stay with a member of parliament in the Isle of Wight. There he was visited by Shaftesbury and Mazzini, and there Tennyson, the Poet Laureate, made him plant a memorial tree and listened to him reciting his favourite poem, Foscolo's *I Sepolcri*. At the request of Admiral Seymour, he also went to see the naval base at Portsmouth, being carried in an admiralty yacht, and manœuvres and firing by the whole squadron were staged for his benefit.

When Garibaldi left for London, it was in a special train. At a rough estimate there were half a million people lining the streets of the capital, and the crowds had been waiting all morning. Nothing like it had ever been seen before, and it was certainly a more triumphant welcome than any other visitor to England had ever received. The carriage took six hours to make the three-mile tour from the station to the Duke of Sutherland's house, where he was to stay. Friendly societies, temperance societies, radical politicians, trade unions, and the Working Men's Garibaldi Demonstration Committee all helped to make up the procession, along with the Duke's private fire brigade. Herzen noted that there were none of the usual scenes of drunkenness and pocket-picking, for the people knew that this was their own special festival. It was an extraordinary and memorable occasion.

Some important figures disapproved of the whole business. The Queen, for one, was "half-ashamed of being the head of a nation capable of such follies"; *The Times*, for another, reckoned it tasteless and plebeian; and Karl Marx, whose idea of revolution was quite different from Garibaldi's, considered what he

saw "a miserable spectacle of imbecility". Almost alone
among the Tories, Disraeli refused all invitations to
meet this pirate. Louis Napoleon was both disgusted
and worried, for he assumed that Garibaldi had been
sent for by the English government "to be held up as
a menace to Europe". Lord Clarendon, who had witnessed the triumphal progress, reassured the Emperor.
It had been a grand spectacle:

> "grand because it was entirely the doing of the
> working classes who looked upon Garibaldi as a real
> hero because he had risen from their own rank of
> life . . . and because he was poor. . . . The people
> had kept order for themselves without police or
> soldiers, they delighted to conduct their hero to the
> house of a Duke and to see him taken by the hand
> by the aristocracy."

For a fortnight Garibaldi became one of the
fashionable events of the London season, as the politicians and aristocracy tried to lionize their unsuspect-
ing victim. When he visited the House of Lords,
bishops competed for the honour of a short conversation with him. Twice he attended the opera. Florence
Nightingale, who was not at home even to royalty,
besought him to visit her incognito. At a civic reception in the Guildhall he drank the traditional loving-
cup and was made a freeman. The future Edward
VII, then Prince of Wales, hurried to London to call on
him, daring the Queen's grave displeasure. He dined
with Gladstone, and lunched with Lord John Russell,
the foreign minister. He had breakfast at the Reform
Club, and was banqueted in the luxurious surround-
ings of Fishmongers' Hall. At a lunch in his honour
the band of Her Majesty's Life Guards played Italian
patriotic music, and once he astonished everyone by

smoking unconcernedly in the private boudoir of one of the first ladies in the land. All these activities were the prerogatives of a privileged person.

Even the prime minister gave him a dinner, having determined in advance to cross-examine him thoroughly and give him some unsolicited advice on politics. The two had an hour's private talk together, and when Garibaldi emerged he was red in the face. Palmerston evidently counselled that revolution in Venice should be delayed, and Garibaldi had retorted that it was never too soon to break the chains of slaves wherever they were.

Almost all the eminent public figures of England seemed intent on being in the craze. Garibaldi patiently kept up an actor's pose, despite all the boredom and his distaste for receptions and long public meals. Unwontedly tactful and astute, he was at once the true-hearted hero and also the courteous gentleman, striking a happy mean between modesty and dignity. For it was always to be hoped that through his own reputation the Italian cause would gain in sympathy and perhaps something more.

Everything was therefore done that was proper. He went to Windsor and called at Eton College for three cheers from the young gentlemen. He was shown over model farms, but had to decline the gift of a steam plough because it would be useless amid the rocks of Caprera. He laid a wreath on Foscolo's tomb at Chiswick. He went, as did all visitors to England, to the brewery of Barclay and Perkins and there drank to the workers of the world in a way that offended some of his sponsors who were not workmen or who had views against liquor. He posed for portraits, sculpture, and photographs. And thus his cult grew and multiplied, from the aristocratic wives who leaned on his arm and professed their undying love, to the ser-

vants at Stafford House who sold bottles of soapsuds
from his washbasin. Whenever possible he flattered
his hosts, praising their police and their love of law
and liberty, and proclaiming himself an Englishman
at heart and proud to be so.

But this artificial life of salons and lunches did not
really please either himself or his radical backers, and
sometimes he broke free from it in a way that led his
highborn hosts to suspect that he might be up to no
good. Some of the English radicals had all along intended to convert his visit into a popular demonstration
against Louis Napoleon and English Toryism. They
disliked the way he had been captured and stifled in
the stuffy atmosphere of fashionable London, and they
found him more than ready when they advised breaking out from the narrowly insulated official routine.

Garibaldi thus went to meet some of the early
trade-union leaders; and one speech records him as
saying that he wanted to see more of the ordinary
workers, "that class to which I have the honour to
belong and who are my brothers all over the world".
Officialdom would have found this unexceptionable,
but not so when at the Crystal Palace he made un-
guarded references to a war against France, nor when
he was visited by a deputation from Denmark, for the
Danish frontier was then the most sensitive spot on
the map and a war was in progress that might easily
have involved the rest of Europe. Later he assured
Speranza von Schwartz that he had really gone to
England to obtain help for the Danes of Schleswig-
Holstein against the invasion by Austria and Prussia.
This must have been greatly embarrassing to the
British government.

He had a number of talks with Mazzini, and at one
private dinner, attended by the most celebrated
European agitators in exile, he proposed Mazzini's

health in a speech that told of his admiration and affection for this arch-revolutionary. Nobody knew what these two might have been hatching together in their unintelligible Genoese patois. Palmerston was certainly worried and made further inquiries. Garibaldi explained that, "had he found Mazzini in prosperity, he would have avoided all misunderstanding by not seeing him; but finding him in adversity, he could not throw him aside". This was truly generous, but perhaps not altogether politic.

When Garibaldi suddenly left England for Caprera, his departure was blamed on the British government, which was said to have disapproved of his radical and lower-class associations and his dangerous involvements on behalf of Denmark and against France. But the matter is more complicated.

Many powerful groups had been against his English journey from the start. Louis Napoleon was horrified when Garibaldi paid a visit to that dangerous agitator Louis Blanc. The corps of ambassadors, excepting only the representatives of the United States and Turkey, had boycotted the whole tour. The Italian ambassador in particular, exceeded in this only by the Austrian ambassador, showed clearly that his government disapproved, and many of the respectable Italian citizens in London followed his lead.

Some of the English liberals—for instance Gladstone, who had close contacts in Turin—were certainly pained by his Mazzinian leanings, and both Gladstone and the Protestants were distressed by his "attenuated belief". The Catholics, through Manning the future Cardinal, proclaimed their disgust at the Archbishop of Canterbury's attendance at a reception in honour of this "representative of the socialist revolution of Italy and of theories which I need not describe". Manning explained that in saying this he was not arguing as a lover of absolutism; nevertheless, all Catholics would feel obliged to remonstrate when Cabinet ministers and peers shamelessly honoured this champion of the lost and wicked cause of Italian unification.

The British government, which had been genuinely surprised by the popular enthusiasm, was furthermore under direct political pressure not to let his visit continue too long or too unrestrictedly. From France, from Belgium, from Italy came pointed protests. Queen Victoria herself strongly objected to her ministers so obviously favouring a man who was a rebel against his own government. But the chief protest came from Italy. Henry Elliot wrote home from Turin of the "extreme irritation and annoyance" there which "it is hopeless to try to appease". Garibaldi's welcome in England was actually weakening the Italian government, and, moreover, at a vulnerable moment when foreign observers were writing of an intense hatred between Left and Right in Italian politics. Opposition victories in by-elections were attributed to this welcome. So was the widespread rioting of students against new examination regulations which at this very moment was compelling the closure of universities up and down Italy. "The government is certainly shaky, and for the moment everything that goes wrong is attributed to the Garibaldian reception."

For these reasons Palmerston cannot have been too happy when it was announced that Garibaldi had accepted almost fifty invitations from other cities in England to repeat his London furore, and that more invitations were still coming in. Liberals everywhere —for example, the Regius Professor of Modern History at Oxford University—had already arranged an elaborate programme of entertainment on this triumphant tour of the provinces. But the official reaction was that these further visits would turn out to be both an anticlimax and a source of permanent political anxiety. Half a dozen large provincial cities would surely be enough for him, especially as there was medical opinion that his health was already suffering from the excitement.

Gladstone himself, the Chancellor of the Exchequer, was called in to persuade Garibaldi that he should keep his provincial tour within limits. This was a delicate task, and was badly bungled. Linguistic difficulties apart, Gladstone was too roundabout and gentlemanly to make himself perfectly clear. Garibaldi understood from what was said that his presence was no longer desired, and he suddenly made up his mind to leave England altogether. He was pressed to think again, for that had not been the intention, but he would not give way. He had at length realized that none of the hoped-for political support was forthcoming; he was exhausted by late nights and bored by protracted social activities in which he understood little; and the further suspicion that he might now be an embarrassment, or even that his revolutionary designs might be suspected, was most unwelcome.

Another small factor was that Menotti and the rest of his personal entourage did not like London. They had been boarded out separately in a cheap hotel, and had not been asked to most of the festivities. Often they were able to see Garibaldi only because he rose at 5.30 a.m., three hours before his first engagement. Perhaps this helps to explain why Guerzoni and the rest spread abroad the wounding suggestion that the English had pressed him to leave forthwith, a suggestion that Garibaldi at the time publicly contradicted.

One engagement only he still kept: a visit to his old companion in arms Colonel Peard, in Cornwall. On his way through the West Country there were tremendous scenes, and railway stations on the way

were crowded all night long in expectation. From
Cornwall he issued a statement full of praise for the
law and order and liberty he had found in England,
for her self-confidence, and for her lack of "that disease
of the times which goes under the unpleasant name
of militarism". After this polite farewell he sailed from
Fowey to a salute of guns, and the Duke of Sutherland's yacht carried him back to the Mediterranean.

No doubt he had failed to win anything positive or
practical in his visit, but one could hardly deny that
in every other way it had been an astonishing success.
It is certainly a bizarre and illuminating incident in
his life, just as it is also a curious comment on the life
of Victorian England.

CHAPTER FOURTEEN

WAR FOR VENICE

1865-1866

ONE other reason why Garibaldi left England in such
a hurry is that Victor Emanuel was sending him messages about starting another war of liberation against
Austria. First a colonel and then a full general had
arrived in London with the suggestion that he should
take an expedition to Galicia and attack Austria in the
rear.

It was an odd proposal, for such an expedition can
have had little chance of success, and the other radical
leaders strongly advised against it. Mazzini, in particular, had already experienced the trickery behind
such royal machinations. He knew that Victor

Emanuel was more fertile in wild schemes than in practical help, and that usually there were selfish or dynastic aims concealed behind this superficial appearance of disinterested patriotism.

The King's motives were probably mixed. No doubt he wanted to coax Garibaldi back from England, where he was having too great a triumph and seemed to be overtopping the Throne itself. In England this overmighty subject was positively dangerous, but if sent off to eastern Europe the man would probably lose some of his reputation and cease to be such a nuisance. It could be assumed that Garibaldi would readily take responsibility to act if given the vaguest assurances from the Court, and would hand over any gains he might secure, while at the same time he would loyally expect to be disowned in case of failure. For an irresponsible man like Victor Emanuel, it was too great a temptation to have a servant who would obediently take all the hard knocks and surrender the profits, and one more tragedy was nearly generated from this fact.

The King was once again trying to make his own policy distinct from that of his ministers. He longed to be something more than a constitutional king—not a mere symbol, but a leader in his own right—and perhaps Garibaldi's success had gone to more heads than one. Victor Emanuel had already clashed with most of his ministers over definition of the sovereign's powers. Several prime ministers had been dismissed out of hand with no reference to parliament, and there had been numerous threats of resignation. It was a painfully weak point in the constitution. Wherever in Europe the transition from absolute to limited monarchy was made, this transitional period was always a phase of difficult adjustment which needed plentiful tact and firm traditions and a well-diffused education in political know-how—more, at least, of each of these than was currently available in Italy.

Soon after Garibaldi's return in May 1864, the same mysterious Colonel Porcelli who had found him in London arrived with another private message from the King. Not a word was said to anyone of what had passed between them, but the chief Garibaldians were forthwith summoned to Ischia for a council of war. Garibaldi himself sailed to this island in the Duke's yacht, which was still waiting for his use.

The rendezvous was chosen partly because he wished to take the mud baths for his arthritis. He was clearly ill at this time and had to ask people not to visit him, and health reasons were also given for his resignation from the grand-mastership of the free-masons. Perhaps his English experiences had, after all, been too taxing.

His lieutenants arrived, stubbornly fixed against any idea of a revolution outside Italy. They reminded him that the King had private interests which were not always those of Italy. For example, there was a project to find a throne in the Balkans or elsewhere for the monarch's second son, the Duke of Aosta (the same who in 1870 became King of Spain), and the revolutionaries might thus find themselves merely a catspaw in a purely dynastic intrigue. In order to prevent Garibaldi from undertaking this Galician scheme, somebody let the device leak into the newspapers, and the King hurriedly called off the whole affair. Garibaldi's secretary, Guerzoni, was dismissed for this inspired journalistic indiscretion, and responded by fighting a duel with the royalist agent Porcelli.

For some time afterwards Garibaldi lived quietly enough at Caprera. He had a finely furnished yacht of his own now, the *Princess Olga*, made of teak at Cowes and presented by English admirers. But he could not afford its upkeep, nor had he any longer the health or inclination for sea voyages. The ship mouldered away at anchor, and after a few years he sold it to the government at what he complained was a vast profit to some middleman.

The various pronouncements he made in the next eighteen months show that his ideas and interests continued to be much the same, albeit their expression became sharper and more acidulous. Often he bewailed the sorry condition of Italy after all the fine hopes he had nurtured. It was a tale of poverty at home, shame and humiliation abroad, while the Italians themselves were poorly educated and physically inferior to the German race. "The day in which our peasants will be really educated, tyrants and slaves will no longer be possible"—this was his hope for the future, but it was a distant prospect .

In the meantime, Garibaldi had no use for parliament and tried not to let his candidacy as a representative go forward. His immediate thoughts were fastened on national liberation—if not of Venice from Austria, then perhaps of Nice from France. In 1865 his restlessness reached the point of debating whether to go to fight for Mexican independence against the Emperor Maximilian, for he espied an alter ego in Benito Juárez, the Mexican revolutionary after whom Benito Mussolini was named a few years later.

One special request he made to the King: to be given full powers and allowed to govern the south as he had done until Cavour bundled him out of Naples in November 1860. There he put his finger on the weakest spot of all. The attempt since 1860 to govern the south from remote Turin had produced a running civil war and a widespread desire to regain Sicilian and Neapolitan independence. "The government is now more hated there than were the Bourbons," wrote

Garibaldi, "and the day war breaks out against Austria
there will be a cataclysmic revolt against us all over the
south." His prophecy was not far wrong. Of course the
King had good reasons for not daring to appoint this
dangerous individual a virtual dictator of the south;
yet Garibaldi had shown in 1860 that a picturesque
and generous idealist might hold the affection and
allegiance of the south better than the unimaginative
bureaucrats who had replaced him.

In 1866 the long-awaited day arrived when another
war captured Venice from Austria. Italian morale badly
needed a momentous victory to seal and justify the
national revolution. For this purpose, armament-pro-
duction had been made the largest item of the
country's expenditure, and a fearful burden of taxes
was imposed in order to produce the transient euphoria
of military success. It was a sensitive point that Lombardy had been the gift of Louis Napoleon, Naples and
Sicily the gift of Garibaldi, Tuscany and Romagna the
gift of those Central Italians who had insisted on being
annexed. What was sorely needed was a notable feat
of arms to establish that Italy was now a great nation,
and so to turn the prose of national life into poetry.

At last in 1866 advantage was taken of Bismarck's
successful provocation of war. Bismarck was interested
only in asserting Prussian supremacy over Austria in
Germany, but he was glad to have an ally who would
divide the enemy's forces. Austria offered to cede
Venetia at once provided that Italy stayed out of the
war, but the government had in mind to conquer
Italian-speaking Trieste and the Tyrol as well, and so
refused. Garibaldi was deliberately made to stay well
out of the picture as long as possible. He was told that
he could again command a unit of volunteers, but until
the last moment he was compelled to stay at Caprera

so that he should have no say in organizing the men he was to command or in planning strategy.

Some people later maintained that the whole preparation and conduct of the war were so faulty that it would not have mattered much what strategic plan had been adopted. The King privately sent advance word to Caprera that the volunteers would most likely be landed on the Dalmatian coast, this being a scheme that fitted in with the German plan of campaign and particularly appealed to the volunteers. Garibaldi liked the idea of a remote and independent command where he would not have to co-operate with other generals and fit into a larger pattern. He also preferred a revolutionary war, and counted on a Slav rebellion against Austria in the Adriatic area. So he lost no time in preparing maps and sending people to organize revolution on the spot.

The plan was then suddenly changed, and instead he was ordered to the Tyrol. General Lamarmora, who now was prime minister, decided not to risk anything like a revolutionary war of popular insurrection, nor to pay any heed to the German strategical plans. He wanted Italy to fight her own distinct war, and to stake all on a frontal attack against the quadrilateral of fortresses on which Austria relied for her power in northern Italy. Few people have been found subsequently to justify his decision.

On June 10, just before war began, Garibaldi was allowed to leave Caprera. He was greatly excited at the prospect of fighting once more. In accordance with regulations, he again cut off much of his beard and hair. He had been convinced that at least 100,000 volunteers could be mustered, but Lamarmora allowed him only 35,000 and nearly half of these were kept down in the heel of Italy, far away from the front. They were permitted to wear their red shirts, but once

K

more their arms were inferior to those of the regular troops—museum pieces, it was said—and the delays in recruitment and organization led Garibaldi to think that again there were political reasons for not letting the irregulars steal the limelight and the applause. For the volunteer army had become closely associated with the Left, and the regulars with the conservative Right to which General Lamarmora belonged.

Garibaldi established his headquarters at Salò on Lake Garda. Great difficulties were experienced in suddenly starting up his volunteers from scratch again, appointing officers, training the men, forming an administration, and working out all the requisite regulations. The special nature of irregular warfare had to be studied by all, at least in its rudiments. Various commando groups had to be formed by the swiftest and boldest in each regiment, who would go off on their own and cut railways and electricity installations behind the enemy lines.

The basic lessons to be learned can be seen from the instructions issued. These stated that the chief danger for volunteer units was sudden infectious panic, and anyone who showed fear had therefore to be given a good drubbing. Engagements by small groups were to be undertaken only with great caution, for even small defeats might prove disastrous to morale, and great pains should be taken never to leave the wounded behind to be captured by the enemy. Volunteers always needed to know the reason for everything, and officers should take care to explain the why and wherefore of success and defeat. Careful and repeated instruction must impress on all that the greatest losses were sustained in fleeing from the enemy, while "among really brave men few are killed and victory is always won". Irregulars should learn to attack not *en masse*, but in open formation. They should always seize any high points of vantage before attacking a strongly defended position. Equipment must be kept perfectly clean, and all ranks should take frequent baths in the lake.

The Italians had a great superiority in numbers to the forces that Austria could use on her southern front, but were poor in equipment and generalship. The King thought that he had a natural gift for strategy, and sometimes interfered too much. The two commanders, Cialdini and Lamarmora, were intensely jealous of each other, and often went their own ways without co-ordination. The basic strategic conception was almost certainly wrong, and a long, straggling front was established against fortresses from which the enemy could easily choose where to concentrate.

After preliminary feints, the Austrian attack came on the Italian left. In a matter of days a minor defeat at Custoza sent the main Italian army reeling back for thirty or more miles without even being pursued, leaving the whole of Lombardy wide open. It was a terrible blow to the confidence of the troops. This was followed by a naval defeat at Lissa, again a culpable business in which twelve ironclads were beaten by seven, and superior numbers were outclassed by infinitely greater skill and better discipline. Garibaldi, himself an experienced admiral, had bitter words over this. There was excellent material in Italian crews, but he lamented that the officers were selected by nepotism from a privileged class. Count Persano, the admiral commanding at Lissa, was a case in point, and it was not much consolation that he was now impeached before the Senate and condemned by his peers to lose rank and pay.

The only memorable Italian victory in 1866 was won by Garibaldi, and this is the more remarkable in that he was no longer the dashing captain, but was rheumatic and ageing, and that a light wound had compelled him to direct operations from a carriage litter. Nor were his men quite the same as of old. After 1860 the best volunteer generals had joined the regulars, and the rank and file had been under discipline for only a few days. Their lack of coats against the mountain cold and rain, and their want of rifled precision weapons made them the laughing-stock of an enemy well practised in Alpine warfare. But this time the Garibaldians were superior in numbers, and their courage was the same as ever. Austria, moreover, had been heavily beaten by the Prussians at Sadowa, and so was in no mood to be aggressive on her southern front. The volunteers placed a trust in Garibaldi which was complete and unquestioning. In his soft, insinuating voice, said one of them, there lay all the authority of a Cæsar, and never a single man dared answer or contradict him openly.

There was some private criticism at the time of his direction of the Alpine campaign, especially for allowing his opponents to impose their own plan. But he had little room for deployment in this kind of battle area, and the fact remains that Garibaldi did push the Austrians back until he commanded the two valleys leading up from Lake Garda to the town of Trent. Particularly in capturing the village of Bezzecca his tactical sense was the decisive factor. Even though he could not properly observe the ground from his carriage, his arrival immediately retrieved a difficult situation; he at once sensed where to place his artillery and what were the more important points that had to be taken. Thus he stopped an Austrian movement down the valley, and instead opened the way into the Tyrol. Just at this very point the Prussians called off the war—from which they had gained all that they wanted—leaving Italy to escape as best she could.

In the upshot Italy won Venice, though Austria would not cede this province directly to an enemy whom she had beaten so convincingly at Custoza and Lissa; instead, she disdainfully gave it to France, who passed it over as second-hand goods to Victor Emanuel. Any hope of obtaining Trieste and Trent had to be abandoned, and so Italy's north-eastern frontier was still left wide open and evidently indefensible. It all seemed to have been a useless waste of lives, because Austria had offered to surrender Venice before war had even begun. The newly established united kingdom was easily liable to feelings of humiliation over such an outcome, especially when, hard on top of defeat, ministers and generals began wrangling in public over whose fault it had been.

Nor was Garibaldi exempt from this wrangling. He had been within sight of Trent when told that there was an armistice and that he must withdraw, and in his briefest style he had replied: "I obey." But the same day, August 9, he issued a caustic proclamation to the volunteers blaming his superiors for what had happened. Therein he recited the "Jesuitical treatment" he had received, the broken promises to give him adequate supplies, and the political animosity against his irregular force.

What wounded most was that the mountain villages had not risen to help turn out the Austrians as he had expected. Perhaps Venice, under an Austrian garrison, could be forgiven for not showing any manifest excitement as her liberators drew near, but not even in the silence of the countryside had any action been taken against isolated enemy soldiers hurrying away with their booty. A free and regenerated Italy was apparently the last thing that the common people wanted, and their apathy showed that they were hardly worthy of being forced to be free. Not a single peasant had volunteered to fight. Evidently the most vigorous and hard-working—and by far the most numerous—class of Italians considered itself neutral, or even on the enemy's side.

CHAPTER FIFTEEN

DEFEAT AT MENTANA

1867

THE next chapter in Garibaldi's history contains one of his few military defeats, all the more painful for being at the hands of France and the Papacy.

He was sixty years old in 1867. During the previous two years his hair had noticeably thinned and become white, and his pallid face reflected pain and suffering and what someone recorded as precocious old age. But his dress remained exactly the same, with the inevitable red blouse and usually the embroidered cap that one of his women friends presented to him each year. And, underneath, his spirit was as excitable and mettlesome as ever.

Early in 1867 Garibaldi left Caprera again to campaign for some of his Leftist acquaintances in the elections. He wanted a clean sweep of the old representatives because the shame of Custoza and Lissa lay indisputably at the door of parliamentary corruption and sycophancy. It was strange to find him much concerned over elections, and it shortly became clear that he was simply using the campaign as an excuse to work up enthusiasm for the conquest of Rome. His candidate friends were soon trembling in their shoes

wondering what he would say next, because his pre-
occupation with Rome had become an obsession.
Regrettably, Italians were beholden to Prussia for
Venice—this was the burden of his song—and only an
overwhelming popular movement for Rome would
now wash out the mortification of defeat; only a native
Italian insurrection would establish that the nation was
something desirable and desired, instead of just an
artificial creation of circumstances and the concert of
Europe. This was the message that Garibaldi delivered
in each successive city from the window or balcony
of his hotel, and a tremendous personal reception
deceived him into thinking that everyone was waiting
for him to give the word.

In these same speeches his political animus against
the Vatican was also linked up with remarkable phrases
about a new revelation, a new natural religion of
Christ which dispensed with priests and altars and
doctrine. Apparently he had appreciative audiences
for these, too, and the applause gave him the further
illusion that a religious revival was starting with himself as its prophet, a religion in which everyone would
instinctively help the unfortunate and fight against all
tyrants whether political or spiritual. This became
ridiculous when he presumed to baptize infants
brought to him in the name of God; and yet few people
were moved to outright laughter. It says much for his
prestige that he could flourish on this kind of behaviour; it also says much that the small electorate
of well-to-do were ready to elect him and yet elected
none of the sixty other candidates he had recommended. Rattazzi returned to power as premier, the
man of Aspromonte.

Garibaldi's immediate aim was not religious but
political: to turn the Pope out of Rome. He reminded
people that full powers had been conceded him in

1849 by the elected republican assembly in revolutionary Rome, and by virtue of these powers he formally protested against that "pestilential institution" the Papacy. Justice and international law were invoked against the "negation of God" now ruling in Rome, and the Pope's government was boldly declared illegal. This was in March 1867.

Ricciotti Garibaldi was now ordered to collect money in Protestant England, and a military campaign fund received a large contribution from the rich Tuscan financier Adriano Lemmi who had underwritten most of Mazzini's insurrections. A proclamation called on all patriotic women to recommence making red shirts. Contact was established with revolutionary committees in Rome, and the Romans were rebuked for not having risen when the French garrisons had been withdrawn a few months earlier. There was even a deputation from Rome which came to see Garibaldi in June. Credulous as always, he did not penetrate behind their flowery rhetoric, but simply assumed that these would-be revolutionaries meant what they said. He could always believe what he wanted to believe, and often failed to remember the type of person he was dealing with. The conviction took root in his mind that people were irremovably fixed on a revolutionary war for Rome.

In early September Garibaldi suddenly appeared at a congress in Geneva held by the International League of Peace and Liberty. People who travelled with him through Switzerland noticed that he was a little surprised and hurt not to receive more fervent popular demonstrations; though still modest and self-effacing by temperament, he had learned to expect applause as his due. Switzerland did not please him this time. Evidently there was not much to choose, after all, between Protestantism and Catholicism. Nor was he much pleased with the congress; he stopped only long enough to give the delegates a hurried lecture on how to solve all the problems of the world, and then decamped, leaving an angry buzz of controversy and indignation behind him.

Their aims, he told the congress, should be, first, to destroy despotism everywhere; second, to abolish war; third, to introduce democracy as the only effective remedy against war. The Papacy should be formally wound up, and the congress should adopt "the religion of God—that is to say, the religion of truth and reason", which meant that the old priesthood of revelation should yield place to a priesthood of science and intelligence. An international body should be formed to judge all issues between nations, and its members should be chosen democratically by the people. Perhaps Garibaldi did not expect such a programme to be endorsed. At all events, he did not wait even for its discussion. He always felt out of place in assemblies where he was surrounded by men cleverer and more loquacious and argumentative than himself. In any case, it was again time for deeds rather than words, and an insurrection was under way for the capture of Rome.

The degree of government complicity in the expedition that led to Mentana is again hard to establish, but it is worth some discussion because the whole affair shows a degree of incompetence and irresponsibility in officialdom which goes far to explain and justify Garibaldi's conduct. He told a friend that he would never have dared to march on Rome with so small a force if he had not been driven on by emissaries of the Italian government; he had been assured that "a few shots into the air" would be enough to provoke a revolution, and that the Italian army would then use this as an excuse to invade on the pretence of restoring order. This was Garibaldi's story, though possibly it may have been an exaggeration or even a half-conscious fabrication; any hints made to him would quite likely have been sufficiently vague to lead (whether on purpose or not) to misunderstanding.

The government's policy certainly appeared to be quite as hesitant and contradictory as at the time of Aspromonte. Rattazzi would no doubt have favoured, and possibly even backed, a genuine revolution inside Rome, but could not be enthusiastic over a Garibaldian invasion that might allow Europe to call the rising a put-up job. Possibly the prime minister underestimated Garibaldi's determination and assumed that the government could always assert itself if necessary and stop the revolt. Perhaps he was just trying to gain time, or waiting to see how successful it was. Perhaps he was afraid of the strength of public opinion, and feared that he might seem a puppet of France if he stood out too obviously against the national movement. We have the evidence of General Cialdini that the state of public opinion now made impossible any government that did not first come to terms with Garibaldi.

At all events, there was no unqualified veto by Rattazzi, and certainly there was a degree of half-hearted connivance. One of Garibaldi's leading officers paid a number of private visits to the chief of police, and seems to have been assured by him that the government might support a revolution. Some of Garibaldi's rifles came from government stores, with evident permission from the authorities. One suspects that Elliot was not far wrong when he wrote:

"The Italian Government shows great want of courage in dealing with these schemes, for they are so afraid of being accused of damping the ardour of the patriots, that they allow themselves to be taken into a sort of half confidence which gives them the appearance of being parties to schemes of which they really disapprove. They have not yet discovered the way to meddle with pitch and still keep their fingers clean."

Once again, this was an attempt to follow Cavour's policy without Cavour's finesse.

Garibaldi took no account of these vacillations. He assumed that the government would not and could not stop him, and that any contrary indications were a smoke screen to deceive the rest of Europe. Precisely the same assumption had been made very successfully in 1860 when he set out with the Thousand; after much repetition, the whole complicated farce was becoming a familiar routine.

This time, however, things turned out wrongly, for Rattazzi was too subtle and changeable to hold a consistent course. In the very early hours of September 24 Garibaldi was arrested not many miles from the Papal frontier. The news was greeted with protests and tumult, especially as there was the good pretext that the arrest was in violation of a deputy's immunity. Even when shut up at Alessandria, the victim managed to harangue his guards and was greeted by them with shouts of "To Rome!" Jessie White came to visit him in prison, bringing the portable bathtub which he had left behind in his haste and which was one of his most indispensable articles of personal furniture. To her he gave angry letters of protest claiming naturalization and protection from the ministers of both Great Britain and the United States, saying that he would not remain a citizen of a country whose government behaved as badly as Italy's.

The prisoner was packed off hurriedly to Caprera, as Rattazzi dared not bring him to trial, and incarceration in the insalubrious prison of Alessandria was

notoriously tantamount to sentence of death. Caprera
at the time was in quarantine for cholera, so escape
would not be easy. But, to be quite sure, as many as
nine warships spent the next few weeks enforcing a
blockade, and this was no small part of the Italian
navy.

Doubtless Rattazzi's primary intention of ordering
this close imprisonment was not to end the revolution,
but rather to prove to Europe that any further insurrection in the Papal states would be spontaneous because
Garibaldi had an enforced alibi. Crispi's letters and
diary show that behind this false pose the government
went on giving money and helping the organization of
volunteers. A "spontaneous" insurrection would provide the King with an excuse to cross the frontier in
order to keep law and order. Garibaldi must have
known all about this, and he helped by giving secret
instructions that the *Putsch* should continue without
him under his son Menotti.

At the beginning of October several bands irrupted
into Papal territory, though the Romans remained
impassive and so rendered the whole escapade
thoroughly implausible. At this horrifying news of
local indifference, Rattazzi would probably have drawn
back if he could, but it was too late. The Cairoli
brothers and their band of gun-runners were over the
frontier. And Garibaldi, whom Crispi and Rattazzi
both wanted to stay at Caprera and keep up
appearances, was receiving from other sources word
that the government was backing down, hence he
should escape and head the revolt himself. The only
hope now for the revolutionaries was to compromise
the administration. Possibly the government could be
forced to invade Papal territory, either to support the
revolt, or even to crush it and then annex these new
provinces.

Garibaldi was particularly proud of his escape from Caprera, more than of many more notable actions of his life. Lemmi paid for a small boat which ran the blockade to a neighbouring island. Then Garibaldi, with his beard stained black, leaving a friend to impersonate him walking the terrace on crutches, escaped past the waiting warships in a storm and reached Mrs. Collins's house on Maddalena, where he stayed overnight. A long ride on horseback, and a boat journey past Monte Cristo, and they reached the carriage waiting for them near Leghorn.

On October 20, he was in Florence, which had recently succeeded Turin as the national capital and centre of government. No one dared set hand on him, not even when he addressed the crowd outside Santa Maria Novella. In a provocative speech, he cited the United States as an example of a nation that had fought gloriously to become the freest and most powerful in the world. Borrowing a phrase from one of his heroes, he issued a statement that "Italy expects every man to do his duty". An observer commented that the Florentines were none the less unmoved. Everyone was waiting to see whether the government was behind him.

There is little doubt that Rattazzi had hoped to use these events to blackmail Louis Napoleon into letting Italy have Rome. His grossly sophistical argument was that the Pope had no adequate army to deal with these continual revolutions, whereas an Italian government in Rome would find it easy. In order to demonstrate Papal Rome's proneness to revolution, and also to retain the support in parliament of Crispi and the Left, the prime minister had half connived at the small-scale invasion by Menotti and Cairoli which had already taken place. But once the revolution had begun, it would have been impossible for Rattazzi to go into

reverse without exposing his own sharp practice. And
as he did not arrest Garibaldi again, Louis Napoleon,
seeing the Italians playing this double game,
announced the return of French troops to defend the
Pope. Rattazzi could not decide whether to accept or
to challenge this opposition from France, so the King
stepped in once more to take over the government with
a policy of his own.

Victor Emanuel was hardly of the calibre for a royal
dictator: he was too puny a man, and his time and
energy went to more private and personal interests.
But he liked to possess at least the illusion of
governing. When Louis Napoleon sent his troops back
to Rome, the King—so he himself confessed to Paget,
the British minister—decided to try to cover up what
had happened by collaborating with the French
against Garibaldi. In earlier days he would have fought
against France, but now his army was too weak, or so
he said. Earlier he had covertly abetted and incited
the revolution; now he could no longer control it. He
therefore overrode his dilatory ministers and gave
positive orders for Garibaldi's arrest.

Rattazzi thereupon resigned. If what he told Paget
can be believed, he would have preferred war against
France rather than against Garibaldi. But in fact he
dared not go either forward or back, and now had an
excuse to escape by saying that he could not take
responsibility for this imperious royal action. The King,
as always when in difficulties, turned for a new prime
minister to a military man, first Cialdini and then
Menabrea. Rattazzi apparently advised Cialdini to
arrest Garibaldi at once, not having had the courage
to do so himself. But Cialdini actually sought an interview with Garibaldi at Crispi's house, and Crispi
later told parliament that only the disorganization
in the army had prevented this premier-elect from

ordering the national forces to march on Rome forthwith.

Eight days' interim of political crisis followed before a new government could be constituted, and during this time Garibaldi lived a charmed life with every appearance of secret assistance by the authorities. It was a perfect opportunity. While the people were cheering him outside his hotel in Florence, he slipped out of the back door and joined a special train that Crispi had waiting to leave for the Papal frontier. At last an order was dispatched for his arrest, but Crispi sent warning and it only hastened his crossing of the frontier to join Menotti.

As the march on Rome began, a pathetic proclamation was put out containing the presumed information that the barricades were going up in the holy city. Such had no doubt been the plan, but the Roman insurrection that had been ordered to coincide with the invasion proved to be an unostentatious affair. Gregorovius, then in Rome finishing off his great history of the Middle Ages, thought that a rainstorm had washed it out.

The inhabitants of the Papal states were seemingly not over-anxious to join the more highly taxed subjects of Victor Emanuel. The nationalists attributed this fact to a demoralization wrought by centuries of priestly government, but the Pope concluded that his subjects were genuinely satisfied to stay as they were. Probably there was some truth in both interpretations. The invading army conducted itself no better than most invading armies, so perhaps one cannot wonder at its lukewarm reception.

Once again such a hurriedly recruited force inevitably included people of varied quality and background. Their "democratic" sentiments were sometimes a hindrance to discipline, especially as they were led

by untried junior officers. A few were the same good-
for-nothing rowdies and unemployed that in other ages
of history helped to swell the numbers of the *con-
dottieri,* of the *fascisti,* and even of the *partigiani.*
Garibaldi publicly recognized the existence of this
element and of the shameful acts committed.

He was not now the man to stop a crumbling of
morale. There was the usual murmuring about short
rations and the weather. The invasion had been left
until too late in the season, and after the first engagement there was no place for these unpractised and
exhausted soldiers to lie down and rest except in the
mud. Another unkind stroke of fate brought them up
against a second, "unauthorized" group of volunteers
working independently which even cut the railway line
on which Garibaldi's force depended. Then, towards
the end of October, came the news of the French
landing. On top of this, the new prime minister,
General Menabrea, formally disowned Garibaldi and
announced that the national army would pool forces
with the French against them. Italian troops crossed
the frontier "to restore order". This was the unkindest
cut of all, and desertions multiplied at once among
the undisciplined *francs-tireurs.*

Garibaldi had one initial success when he took the
strong town of Monterotondo, but he could not make
up for lack of plan, nor for an improvised and defective
supply system. This was the disadvantage of being a
great tactician who was not simultaneously a great
strategist and staff officer. Still no rebellion broke out
in Rome to assist him, and the peasants of the countryside would not inform him of enemy movements, so
that only the arrival of French troops was needed to
make the whole situation impossible. Enrico Cairoli,
trying to introduce arms into Rome by rail and river,
met a heroic death just under the city walls, but

heroism was not enough. The only sensible policy would now have been retreat, and yet Garibaldi was within sight of Rome and he scorned to abandon the field without a struggle.

The Battle of Mentana took place on November 3. His own men were outnumbered, and by his own confession they did not fight well; but it was a hopeless task. The French lost 2 men killed, the Papalists 30; the Garibaldians lost 1,600 prisoners alone. It was a victory for grapeshot and for the *chassepots* that fired twelve times a minute. At least the French said it was, for they wanted the world to appreciate the strength of their new weapon. They kept secret that it jammed and became too hot to hold in this, its first big test, and that most of the guns had to be turned in at once for thorough repairs.

Garibaldi and the remnant managed to escape back over the frontier into Italy. As a deputy and, as he thought, an American citizen, he naïvely assumed that no proceedings would be taken against him, and he sent a typical telegram with orders that a steamship should be waiting to transport him back to Caprera. The Italian police, however, stopped his special train, and, when he resisted arrest, hauled him forcibly from his seat. This added indignity to injury and insult.

For three weeks he was held in custody, despite a further appeal to the United States consul. Menabrea seems to have hoped that he could be induced to incriminate Rattazzi, but Garibaldi would say nothing. On the contrary, he arrogantly instructed his lawyers to demand damages for wrongful arrest and the punishment of those who had arrested him. To spare the government further embarrassment, he again offered to leave Italy, but once more it was decided that public opinion would not allow either his trial or exile: the angry muttering of the mob reached even

L

to the King's ears through the thick walls of the
Palazzo Pitti.

Garibaldi's feelings may be imagined. Thrice he
had begun his march on Rome, and always the government had half encouraged and then let him down. On
this occasion he used the ugly word *treachery;* the
monarchy had "sold" him to France; the country was
being dragged through the mud by a gang of servile
and cowardly politicians. There is indeed little doubt
that the whole episode put back quite considerably
the education of the country in liberal and responsible
government.

Garibaldi also vented his bitterness on Mazzini, for
—incorrectly—he imagined that this distant exile was
responsible for encouraging the volunteers to desert.
The republican leader had not approved the
Garibaldian expeditions of 1862 or 1867, for he had
foretold failure, and Mazzinian doctrine theoretically
insisted that the Romans must rise and deliver themselves or else be unworthy of deliverance. Up until
1865 Garibaldi had written about Mazzini usually with
kindness and gratitude, despite their many differences.
Now, in the search for a scapegoat, he began to say
things that were cruel as well as untrue.

Never was he free from resentment over the events
of 1867. Perhaps inwardly he felt a little responsible
himself. In his memoirs he glanced over the years 1862
and 1867, preferring to dwell on the defeats of the
national army at Custoza and Lissa rather than on his
own. Defensively he pointed out that Italian politicians
disapproved of his 1867 expedition solely because it
failed, as they had approved that of 1860 only because
it succeeded; this, he said, was bad ethics and bad
politics. To Garibaldi both expeditions were on the
same level; they had both been a fair gamble.

CHAPTER SIXTEEN

AGAINST PAPACY AND EMPIRE

1868-1871

FOR the best part of three years Garibaldi remained in retirement as a virtual prisoner on Caprera. In 1868 he made another of his theatrical resignations from parliament, and again instanced the brutal and unsuccessful policy of the government towards Naples and Sicily. Otherwise, he turned away from active politics, preferring to cultivate his garden and watch his children grow up. Sometimes his ankle wound opened again. His rheumatism also was becoming much worse. He occasionally used crutches for walking, and could not shake hands easily; sometimes he could not even sign his name.

It is noticeable that after Mentana, as had been the case after Aspromonte, his judgements on men and things became more peppery. He distributed his censure liberally against the Pope, against Mazzini, against even Victor Emanuel, and always against parliament and the infamous system of government in Italy. No doubt this in part reflected his own ill-health, though even more it arose from a deep and lasting disillusion. He had been simple-minded in nourishing the expectation that a united Italy would solve so many problems, but then he was by temperament a simple-minded man.

This was not a general cynicism; his enthusiasm and compassion for the common people were unabated, and for individuals like the exiled Bourbon ex-King of Naples he had kind and sympathetic words.

In private life up to the very end, said Alberto Mario, he was the most good-natured and amiable of men. But his faith in politicians and public figures wore increasingly thin as he saw them all tarred with the same brush. He even abandoned the freemasons because they were not "the instrument of morality and popular progress" he had innocently expected. By nature, he was a person to reel violently from one extreme of illusion to another of disillusionment, and though there was never much malice in the resultant vituperation, he felt strongly and was never a man to mince words.

One immediate result of the Papal victory at Mentana was the intensification of Garibaldi's anti-clericalism. He had always fought against the Church, and, as an admirer of Voltaire, his own motto might also have been *"Écrasez l'infâme"*. His own parents had named him Giuseppe after a saint in the calendar, but he named his children after Italian patriots like Menotti, or ancient Romans like Manlius and Clelia, or humanitarian liberators like Lincoln and John Brown. To break free from the clerical stranglehold seemed to him an absolute prerequisite for any development in the country's moral and political education.

No doubt he really was a religious man, although there was more than a little sophistry and naïveté about his religion. He disliked atheism and indifferentism and "miserable materialism". God exists, he said, because a factory implies an architect, a machine a mechanic, movement a regulator. But he could not believe in the "vengeful, angry, unjust and cruel God of the priests". The only priests he would allow were such as Galileo, Kepler, Newton, "the real ministers of God". The Catholic clergy, he used to say, would be better employed draining the Pontine marshes.

Catholicism was bad chiefly in that, clinging to

Rome and the temporal power, the Pope kept Italy disunited. The Church had gone on record in the 1864 Syllabus of Errors against any compromise at all with liberalism. Moreover, the ecclesiastical domination of the educational system accentuated other-worldly things, and omitted due consideration either of science or of physical training and the inculcation of a social conscience towards the poor. Unlike that other and very different anti-clerical, Cavour, Garibaldi would have been delighted to see the Pope accept the British offer and leave Italy for Malta or for somewhere yet more remote. Nor could he credit the idea of infallibility in a man who would soon suffer corruption like the rest of us.

Sometimes, indeed, Garibaldi quite lost his temper with the Vatican, for he seldom held any views with sustained moderation. The government of Rome was now said to be nothing else but the government of Satan. When two revolutionaries in Rome were sentenced to death, he angrily made an empty threat that two priests would be killed in every Italian city by way of reprisal. Towards 1870 these outbursts became more frequent. Revising his memoirs, he replaced the word *God* by the word *Providence,* and *the omnipotent* by *fortune* or *the infinite.* It would be easy to show that this whole attitude was shallow and muddled, but it reveals one facet of his character and must be given due prominence.

There developed in the 'sixties a cult of Garibaldi which, as already told, led him to think of himself as a kind of anti-Pope who could baptize people. Most opinions concurred that he was not a vain man, but of course there was an enormous self-confidence behind his outward humility, and the unprecedented ovations that greeted him often misled a not very subtle or critical mind. This self-deceit was assisted by the fact that he did not have a very pronounced sense of humour. Though he was a good-humoured man and had a radiant smile, one seldom discovers him really laughing, and Jessie White had found that he could never understand a joke. So he himself came to accept his own legend, because he believed too easily what others told him they believed.

The cult of Garibaldi grew up as a boost for national morale, because his own victories stood out sharply from the dreary succession of military defeats between 1848 and 1866. This is another essential facet in his character, that he was the sort of person about whom others romanced, becoming the superhuman projection of events which were heroic, epic, legendary. The people around him had a natural bent towards hero-worship, and some of them, like Dumas and the Baroness von Schwartz, were also romantic story-tellers. Hence the real Garibaldi is sometimes elusive, the cult was sometimes exorbitant, and he himself was encouraged to think that he was somewhat larger than life.

Many relics were preserved to foster the myth—for example, his red shirts (more, one may assume, than he ever wore) and the intimate domestic furniture of rooms in which he slept, the bullet that pierced his ankle, even the bloodstained stretcher that carried him from Aspromonte. His youngest daughter, Clelia, tells how she religiously kept his hair and nail clippings. Popular illustrations of Garibaldi displaced the image of royalty and even of God in many a humble log cabin, and some prints showed him in the act of blessing, or even crucified and ascending. Quite generally in the south he was credited with magical or divine powers, and we find one Roman expecting that he would return to earth in the rôle of Christ the second. In Naples and Sicily, where over ninety per cent of the population was illiterate, he was at once magnified into an idealized symbol of the millenium, and as such his image has down to our own day been dragged into electoral posters, for it is a sure vote-catcher, one that even the uneducated can understand.

There appeared in the 'sixties some printed cate-chisms and prayers that give some idea of the grip he came to hold on popular imagination. They are blasphemous and in poor taste, but then there was a great deal of both about *garibaldinismo*, and there is no doubt that for both Garibaldi and his friends they were something more than merely an inelegant and bad-tempered joke. One of these prayers was pre-scribed for daily use and addressed him as father of the people:

Thy will be done in barracks as on the field of battle. Give us ammunition each day. And do not lead us into the temptation of counting the numbers of the enemy. But deliver us from the Austrians and the priests.

One catechism contained this sort of question and answer:

Q. How does Garibaldi reward those who love Italy?
A. With victory.
Q. What does one gain by victory?
A. The sight of Garibaldi himself and every kind of pleasure without pain.
Q. What are the three distinct persons in Garibaldi?
A. The father of his nation, the son of the people, and the spirit of liberty.
Q. How did he make himself man?
A. He took on a body and soul just like ourselves, in the blessed womb of a woman of the people.
Q. Why did he make himself man?
A. To save Italy.

In addition there was an injunction for frequent prayer
to the saviour. And a new decalogue included such
commandments as:

> Honour the fatherland, that you may inhabit it
> forever.
> Thou shalt not kill, except the enemies of Italy.
> Thou shalt not commit fornication, except against
> the enemies of Italy.
> Thou shalt not covet the national territory of other
> people.

In the enforced idleness of 1868 Garibaldi began
writing his first novel, *Clelia,* and so presented would-
be detractors with one more weapon against his reputation. All told, he wrote three novels, including one
that dealt with the Thousand in Sicily—it is interesting
to see that he thought this expedition needed poetic
treatment and embellishment. He had perceived that
there was a good market for the historical novels of
Manzoni, Dumas, and Hugo, and as people usually
said more than polite things about his own casual
writings, he decided to try his hand at what he hoped
might be a profitable vein. Once again he was the
victim of his own honesty and candour and other
people's flattery.

He artlessly tells us that his reasons for writing
were, first, to earn a living and stave off the pangs of
hunger; second, to remind Italians of their glorious
dead and stir the youth of the country to renewed effort;
and, third, because in this unwelcome retirement he
could live a romantic life only in flights of fancy. He
also thought to find through fiction a wider audience
for his strictures on the Church: for this he now took
to be his chief vocation in view of the ecclesiastical ban
against Italian liberalism and nationalism. He felt him-

self to be competent as a historian, though he had discovered how easy it was to go wrong in re-creating from memory all the events of a battle; but he fairly confessed to doubts about his ability in fiction, and only urgent personal and national needs impelled him to this kind of writing.

The novels are uninteresting except for the little light that they throw on Garibaldi's character. They are romantic tales of love and heroism, and, as one might expect, rhetorical, ingenuous, and digressive. Their plots are both dull and fantastic, barely enlivened by tales of incest and sinful *amours* inside the Vatican. One need only add that a dozen foreign publishers refused to take *Clelia*.

Garibaldi was better at writing proclamations, to which a forceful, declamatory, and bombastic style was more suited. His *pensées* were less immediate and so less thoughtful and sharp than he can have imagined, but may be consulted to find his succinct considerations on government, the soul, woman, and so forth. Of his autobiographical poem in hendecasyllabic verse, the less said the better. He could turn out French and Italian poems of a kind with some facility, and had just a touch of that art of rude improvisation which can still be found occasionally among country folk in Italy, but the quality of his verse was low. His use of metre, incidentally, betrays an imperfect pronunciation of Italian, and his grammar was defective. His elder brother in Philadelphia used to urge him to settle down and learn Italian properly, but Garibaldi acknowledged that he had been an indifferent scholar in this respect.

The *Memoirs* are his best writing for they reflect a real personal excitement, yet even these are studded with digressions and polemical outbursts. As Giuseppe Abba noted of his conversation, Garibaldi's memory

was always poor and unreliable, and it is therefore
possible to see how various recollections were trans-
muted by the course of subsequent events. Later versions became increasingly critical of the monarchy
and Mazzini and the Church. Some of the most gallant
and adventurous scenes that many people thought re-
dounded most to his credit were cut out of the
so-called definitive edition of 1872, and for that reason
the earlier versions are usually favoured, whether
rightly or wrongly.

In 1870 Italians unexpectedly found themselves in
possession of Rome. The Franco-Prussian War had
forced Louis Napoleon to withdraw his protecting
troops, and the Italian army invented a pretext for
invasion and on September 20 brushed aside a merely
token Papal resistance.

Remarkably enough, Garibaldi was not excited, for
he was not personally involved in the fighting, and he
deplored that the great culminating feat of national
unification should have come about in such a casual
backstairs manner. At the time he was in Caprera,
contemplating how he could assist France against those
very Prussians who were making the capture of Rome
at long last possible. This was ironical. And further
irony lay in his wanting to fight for France, the
country that had beaten him in 1849 and 1867. The
fact was that France had now been herself catas-
trophically defeated at Sedan, and had thus aroused all
the inexhaustible sympathy he reserved for what was
oppressed and downtrodden. She had also come into
his good graces politically by overturning the Emperor
and establishing that best of all governments, a
republic.

Thus easily did he cease talking of universal peace
and instead throw himself into the tail end of a major

European war. His own war aims against Prussia he pronounced to be justice and the cause of humanity, both of them complicated and elusive things that he simply assumed he could identify at sight. It was part of Garibaldi's charm that he was seldom troubled by doubt about such matters. His not to count the cost, but to do and, if necessary, to die.

When first he offered "what is left of me" to the French republic, no reply was received. The government was not particularly anxious to have him, and anyhow his offer must have seemed patronizing. But he was not to be put off so easily; this war for republican France against aggressive and imperialistic Prussia he was to call the most important of his whole lifetime.

Fighting like this for a nation other than his own is a good example of that impetuous and generous good nature which many people remembered as Garibaldi's most prominent characteristic, and it also reflects the quixotism and love of the sweeping *beau geste* which were equally in character. He believed all he heard of Prussian brutality in killing prisoners and burning the *francs-tireurs* alive. Also he had an abiding love for the life of battle and companionship in arms. Caprera was lonely, and he felt himself shelved and forgotten while the conservatives monopolized and degraded all public life in Italy.

Objections were thus set aside, and, eluding the Italian navy, he reached Marseilles, where a great reception was waiting. If not governments, at least public opinion appreciated the Hero of Two Worlds. An embarrassed Gambetta tried to palm him off with a small group of several hundred volunteers, but Garibaldi threatened to go home again. This would not have looked well, so with some difficulty a large command was found for him, about five thousand men,

the so-called Army of the Vosges. Menotti and
Ricciotti, now in their late twenties, both had brigade
commands in this army, which was essentially an
irregular force. Their father was cold-shouldered by
the French generals, who resented him as an amateur
and as a foreigner and recent enemy; and mutual re-
sentments continued to make it very hard to integrate
his anomalous group into the rest of the defence.

Garibaldi's military action on the eastern front had
a more symbolic than practical effect on the course of
this short and not very important campaign. He himself was tired and old, now over sixty-three, walking
with a stick and sometimes not able to mount a horse.
This did not prevent him from relying as always on an
offensive strategy, on speed, quick decisions, effrontery
and recklessness, for these were the only tactics he
knew. This time, for a change, he was up against a
first-rate general, yet was not disgraced. It may even
be argued that both in grasp of strategy and in execution he stood out remarkably well in comparison with
his French colleagues. But he was fighting in what was
a lost cause from the start, and the Germans forced
an armistice early in 1871.

No sooner was the war over than this Italian
general was elected to the French National Assembly
in Bordeaux. It may seem odd that a man so averse to
parliaments of every kind should accept a place in a
foreign legislature. However, he wanted for form's
sake to register a public vote for republicanism, since
he could not do this in Italy, and he was keen to show
his solidarity against the new German Emperor who
had just been proclaimed at Versailles. He also felt
under obligation to plead the cause of the Italians who
had been wounded or orphaned in the service of
France.

In February he arrived in Bordeaux, having been

elected in six different places. A storm of protest went up, for the representatives were more staid and less sentimental than the electorate. To the deputies he was still a revolutionary, as he was also a foreigner, an anticlerical, even a socialist. When he found that he could not make himself heard through the shouting, he returned at once to Caprera with what dignity he could muster. Apparently his instinct about the hollowness of parliamentary government had not been so far wrong after all. It was left to Victor Hugo to speak up on his behalf a month later, and to suggest that the animus against Garibaldi was due to the fact that he was the only general on the French side who had been unbeaten in the recent war, the only general to capture a German flag. Victor Hugo himself was shouted down for this public indiscretion, and he, too, went off into exile, disgusted by such ingratitude.

Garibaldi's intervention had not been appreciated. Nevertheless, the episode indicates the genuineness of his internationalism. If he still remained primarily a nationalist, the object of his nationalism was the liberation of peoples and certainly not patriotic aggrandizement. Patriotism was not enough. Freedom and independence had been his paramount aim ever since he first fought for the Rio Grande, the freedom of individuals and nations to exist with a minimum of force on the one hand and a minimum of self-abasement on the other. Any falling short on this principle had not been due to obliquity or ill-will on his part, but simply to obtuseness and faulty analysis. Garibaldi was something of a fool, but nothing of a knave.

CHAPTER SEVENTEEN

LATTER-DAY POLITICS

1872-1881

GARIBALDI in old age never ceased to be a reformer. If anything, the vague Saint-Simonianism of his early years became more pronounced. Not that it simultaneously became much less vague; for it was his nature much less to think than to feel, and his understanding was never acute. The very gusto of his enthusiasm was possible only because he thought and saw superficially. Florence Nightingale had quickly noticed that he did not seem to understand properly the causes he fought for, but always answered her queries with specious and nonsensical abstractions. Criticism of this trait would be beside the point, for starry-eyed idealism was his inner core and the secret of his success. Idealism and a certain amount of simple good sense went together, uncomplicated by subtlety or artifice; but sometimes it was unaccompanied by any refinement of grasp or judgement.

In later life Garibaldi continued to issue manifestos declaring war on war and propagating his doctrine of popular sovereignty. Constantly he criticized the government for the neglect that was making a desert of Sardinia and Sicily, and for imposing the harsh grist tax that fell on the poorest classes who were least able to bear it. Perched on his lonely eminence in Italian society and in his self-imposed exile as a voluntary Robinson Crusoe, he became even more nonconformist and eccentric, beyond criticism and so a law unto himself.

As soon as the term *socialist* came into current usage, he applied it to himself, without any very elaborate views about what socialism meant. In 1880 he wrote to the radical *Secolo* to explain that it was in being socialist that his own republicanism differed from Mazzini's. No doubt this was a genuine difference, because Mazzini once even said he would rather see the Austrians back in Italy than see socialism triumph and create bitter divisions among Italians. Yet the difference is not so large when we find what Garibaldi meant by the term. Socialism for him was nothing very revolutionary, and perhaps he flaunted the word partly because he delighted to feel that it would shock the Mazzinians on the one hand and the complacent conservatives in parliament on the other.

Garibaldi began from the assumption that the social difficulties of Italy were remediable with good will, and were not the result of any intractable or unalterable law—there was little room in his system for original sin. He had far more knowledge of the common people than had Mazzini, and more sympathy with them than had Cavour and the other leaders of united Italy; for by heredity, environment and temperament he understood the masses, and was understood by them. Centuries of unhappy history had instilled into Italy the habit of mind which split rulers from ruled, and had generated a feeling of distrust as though the interests of citizens were diametrically opposed to those of the governing classes. Now Garibaldi laid down the novel and unacceptable doctrine that you must love people in order to rule them; governed *con amore*, they would respond with real enthusiasm. This attitude had seemed to work for the short time that he had been dictator of Naples, when he and his ministers had governed without taking any salary and almost without a police force. Certainly the lack of any similar attitude had something to do with the failure of his successors.

Here was a socialism of the heart and not of the head. In 1875 he wrote to the mayor of Naples that he would like to visit the great southern capital, not to see its beauties, but to go into the hovels and airless cellars where the poor somehow managed to live. He advised the mayor against the giving of alms, for that bred further poverty and destroyed the independence of human personality; what these paupers needed was jobs. This was an authentic compassion, and good sense to boot; and in this particular field neither sense nor compassion was particularly common at the time.

By his own admission Garibaldi was never at home in discussions of high politics, but on such problems of internal social reform he spoke from genuine knowledge and feeling. His suggestions were sometimes far-fetched, but rarely obscure or irrelevant. For instance, he wanted changes in education so that even at the primary levels people should learn not only their alphabet but also technical matters that might be useful in a job. In one little village he tried to find a sponsor for a weekly newspaper to be distributed free to the common people: it would be small, so as to keep expenses down; printed in large type, so as to be read easily; using only simple and popular language and containing but few ideas, lest it prove too severe a tax on simple minds. The general attitude of governments, however, as also of the Church, was that the Press was a dangerous instrument better kept for the few; and, likewise, that education was a precious commodity to be rationed, and preferably limited to literary and non-technical subjects.

The width of Garibaldi's interests and sympathies can be measured by taking a cross-section from his pronouncements in the years 1872-1873. Although realistic enough to see that universal suffrage could not be secured yet, he nevertheless demanded an electoral reform that would extend the franchise to more than the two per cent of Italians who were then permitted to vote, and would thus give ordinary citizens more influence in politics. He asked for disestablishment so that the Catholic Church would lose its privileged monopoly. He wanted to dissolve the monasteries; to introduce free and universal education; to abolish the taxes on such articles of basic necessity as salt and flour, and to introduce a single income tax adjusted to individual wealth. In most of this, he was on the side of the future.

We find him at the same time demanding that the statutory right to free assembly and a free Press should be made less of a mockery than it was in fact. As a good democrat, he insisted that titles ought to be abolished for good. As an experienced general of volunteers, he asked that conscription and a permanent standing army should be replaced by a less expensive form of citizen militia. He also hoped that the state would take over the organization of labour. These were all typical proposals of the Left-wing opposition to the conservative government of Cavour's successors.

Garibaldi's practical sense is shown even in his socialism, as he had little use for the essentially theoretical demands that he said were made by all the leaders of international labour except the English. The doctrinaires wrongly concentrated on vapid generalities like the emancipation of labour, the war of labour against capital, collectivism of the land and of the instruments of production. For such abstractions he had no use at all. In his own private life he found out how difficult it was to regulate on purely theoretical grounds such matters as conditions of work and land

M

tenure. Instead, politicians should fasten on practical ameliorations of the conditions of the underprivileged. The intention should be "to improve human society by gradual and practicable means, and not to waste time or drag ourselves into a social cataclysm which none of us surely wants".

Unlike Mazzini, Garibaldi praised the Paris commune of 1870, partly influenced by the fact that only the revolutionary faction in France had really welcomed his military intervention against Germany. He also formally adhered to the socialist International; but then he said that he had belonged to it since his early South American days, and evidently he meant something different than did many other of its members. He specifically said that he was not opposed to the ownership of capital and the practice of inheritance, nor did he wish to confiscate other people's property just because it was bigger than his; all he wanted was that those with very little property should receive a fair deal and not have the tax system weighted against them.

His socialism was thus brotherhood, humanity, justice, liberty for all, not equality in any sense except equality of opportunity. This was socialism with a difference, based not on class war but on minimizing tension between capital and labour. It was neither rigid nor doctrinaire. Whenever labour acquired capital, said Garibaldi, it would "cross over and side with the employers, so that the elements in the struggle would continually alter by defection". In this belief he was wiser and more perceptive than many others in his generation.

With such advanced views, he was bound to become an unofficial leader of labour, and his biographer, Sacerdote, is no doubt right to claim for him a great influence on the development of democratic and Left-wing movements in Italy. Most organizations like the League of Democracy and the Workers' Fascio included his name among their founders. When the very multiplicity of such bodies became an obstacle to progress, he tried to weld into one *fascio* all the workers' organizations, all the democratic bodies, rationalists, freemasons, mutual-aid societies and the like, which had the betterment of the human situation as their aim. This was too much to hope for, especially in Italy. As soon as Garibaldi moved from diagnosis to the application of a political remedy, his inexperience and utopianism were only too obvious. His comprehension was not sharp; and he was not immune from that which he criticized in others, the inability to come down to brass tacks from rhetorical flights of fancy.

There was to be almost no legislation at all in Italy for social reform, at least not until well into the new century. The governing classes were uninterested in creating restraints for themselves; indeed, one of their basic objects in the *risorgimento* had been to break free of the moral and prescriptive shackles imposed on free enterprise by feudalism and the Church. The radical opposition, for its part, erred in being too visionary and impractical to constitute a proper stimulus to a reformation of manners and morals. Likewise, the divisions among all the various factions of the radical and socialist parties were another obstacle in the path of social reform, and have continued to be so down to the present day.

These divisions inside the Left were a characteristic product of the individualism and anarchism that have disconcerted Italian politics in every age. Mazzini and Garibaldi, for instance, were so near to each other and yet so far from being able to reconcile their highly individualistic natures and programmes. Mazzini saw, in Garibaldi, a potential dictator, a socialist, an ignoramus, a man with a face like a lion and as stupid—so he told John Morley in 1864. The picture was overdrawn but recognizable. From the other side, Garibaldi saw in Mazzini an uncompromising character who insisted on playing his own game, who wasted resources in countless small insurrections but would not support those led by other people, "a man of theory, not of practice, who is always speaking of the people though he does not know who the people are".

Garibaldi pointedly did not attend Mazzini's funeral in 1872, but pursued the republican leader with invective into the grave. Normally a generous man, Garibaldi now stooped so far as to call this greatest of nationalists "an obstacle in the way of Italian unity". He was speaking of the man from whom he had first learned how to be an Italian. This was a notable failure of perception and sympathy in one who seldom lacked at least sympathy, but Mazzini was an intractable bedfellow and few of his associates did not break from him sooner or later.

Another target for Garibaldi's ill-will was the monarchy. Formerly he had trusted the King implicitly; then at an intervening stage he had excused the King as someone misguided by bad advisers; now the same person was pilloried as the man who was chiefly responsible for everything that had gone wrong, and who had hidden the fact behind the doctrine of ministerial responsibility. The 1872 edition of the *Memoirs* excised many of the kinder references to Victor Emanuel. The monarchy was seen to be working for its own selfish and dynastic interests, not for those of the nation. The King was warned that monarchies were not eternal and might be overthrown if they did nothing to deserve the affection of ordinary people.

Garibaldi's politics in the 'seventies were often acid,

petulant, and contrary. He had been elected to all except one of the eight parliaments since 1860, but had seldom taken his seat. Several entire legislatures had gone by without his appearing at all, and he made only a bare dozen parliamentary interventions in all his career. Sometimes he imperiously sent messages to be read in his absence. More than once he demonstratively resigned his seat in protest. Laconic communiqués were issued from Caprera, usually to censure the government for its excessive taxes, its overspending, and its obsequiousness towards foreign states. As he said, people had not voted for these exactions or this subservience when they supported the plebiscites for national unification; in other words, there had been a breach of an implied contract, and this might even absolve subjects from obedience to the laws and institutions of the country.

Only on rare occasions did he now leave Caprera, which fact makes his arrival at Rome in 1875 the more interesting. As his first appearance there since 1849, it caused great excitement. His expenses had apparently been paid in part by contributions from the workers of Milan. The inevitable speech on arriving at his hotel said that he was no orator and would speak little, and he was as good as his word. A visit was paid to the King, and visits were received from ministers who no doubt were curious to know what he had in store for them. The future Imperial German Chancellor, Prince von Bülow, met him often during these days, and recorded that he had "beautiful kind eyes and a very simple manner. There was something naïve, dreamy and yet heroic about him."

Garibaldi attended parliament to sign the register, and there entered his occupation as "farmer". He made one speech on the navy, recommending the construction of bigger and better ironclads. But his chief interest turned out to be nothing more than a project for embanking and diverting the River Tiber. Almost every year there were floods in Rome, every twenty years really dangerous floods. Sometimes two-thirds of the city was under water, and always the summers were rendered unhealthy. He pointed out that malaria had afflicted the King himself and had killed one of Cobden's daughters and one of his own. By making a small deviation in the bed of the Tiber, these floods and malarial swamps could be controlled and one of the largest rivers in Italy could again be made navigable for sizable ships almost up to the capital. Rome might be on its way to a third great period at the head of civilization.

Garibaldi went out personally to take soundings in the river, and one way and another took great trouble over the scheme he presented. His speech on the subject was greatly applauded, and he wrote (or at least put his name to) further long newspaper articles, which were eagerly read. But objections were raised on technical and financial grounds, and he was not well enough to take part in all the debate. Before long he was back again on Caprera, feeling even more frustrated by the slowness and intrigue and vested interests that seemed to be an indispensable adjunct of parliamentary government.

In 1876, before Garibaldi left Rome, the balance of power politics changed radically for the first time, and the Left came to power under his old friend Agostino Depretis, who had been governor of Sicily under him in 1860. Garibaldi's stay in the capital had run him severely into debt, so he made the change of administration an excuse to accept at last the substantial gift that he had hitherto refused from parliament as long as Cavour's party was still in office.

But a year of the Left convinced him that

politicians were all of a piece. Depretis in turn proved
to be rotten, corrupt, extravagant, relinquishing his
former policy of reform now that he was in power,
slavishly polishing the steps of the Throne as all the
others had done, thinly masking a similar tyrannical
autocracy behind the forms of constitutionalism. This
was a further and cruel disillusion. Though elected
again, Garibaldi told his electors that it would be useless for him to appear in parliament any more.

Tyranny always received his censure under whatever guise, and this must be stated clearly before
considering his repeated defence of dictatorship as the
governmental system best suited to Italy in her present
state of development. Dictatorship was not the same
as tyranny, he said, but had been given a bad name
merely because of despots like Caesar, in the same way
that Machiavellism had been given a bad name from
certain adventitious associations of the word. Whereas
in reality Fabius, Cincinnatus, and Machiavelli were
among the great glories of Italy, and it was to be noted
that even Caesar had found his Brutus. The finest
period of Italian history had been during dictatorships;
and in other countries he instanced Washington and
Bolívar, who, though not dictators in name, were
stated to be so in fact. A parliamentary regime, on the
other hand, might be merely a cover for a form of
despotism none the less abhorrent for being concealed.

Deep down, Garibaldi instinctively distrusted the
type of person who got elected to parliaments. At
Rome in 1849, at Turin in 1860 and 1861, at Bordeaux
in 1871, at Rome again in 1875, the parliamentarians
had always been against him. There was a radical
difference between himself and them not only in
principles and background but in technique, for he had
no skill in oratorial dexterity or corridor intrigue.
There were thus good reasons why he and the deputies

should fear each other; and he felt much stronger and more important when addressing the people from his balcony than when speaking to the few elect. Clever lawyers made him feel a fool, and this he could never tolerate or forgive.

In England and Switzerland the representative system might serve admirably, for there people could say that the government belonged to them and not they to the government; but in Italy it was "a prostitution worse than the most open despotism". Even in America he had been shocked to see representatives win votes by standing a free round of drinks. No doubt parliamentary democracy was an ideal or even *the* ideal form of government, but in emergencies a democracy that had a low level of political education might lack the requisite concentration of power to save the state.

When Mahomet II was assaulting Byzantium, five hundred men in the city were disputing whether or not they should use unleavened bread in the communion, and the result was the collapse of a whole civilization. Garibaldi concluded from this that the dispersion of sovereignty among a plurality of people was dangerous. It had been the ruin of the first French republic. It might even cause a break-up of the Italian nation—he noted, for instance, the dangerous continuance of autonomist and separatist feelings in Sicily. Italy lacked what he called, in French, a *robuste et redoutable faisceau*. In subsequent years, long after he first used this phrase, its last word was to acquire a different and more familiar tang, and one cannot help feeling that Garibaldi would have found much to admire in fascism, at least during the middle period of Mussolini's dictatorship.

His own basic political recipe was simple. Until society became less corrupt and egoistical, a temporary dictatorship would be required. A dictator could defend the state externally and purge away any internal impurities. He would be elected by the people, and serve only for a two-year period, during which time he could pack the deputies off home. Parliaments talked and did nothing, and sometimes they were the path along which a tyrant rose to power; hence, the people, once they had found the right person, should not risk interfering again in government until the time came round to elect a successor.

Ironically enough, Garibaldi was here recommending a type of government much the same as that for which he had so condemned Louis Napoleon, for the clear line he sought to draw between despot and dictator was spurious and illusory. It was easy for him to argue that there would be the constitutional check of re-election, but of course this was moonshine. It was simple to say that in the new era of peace no dictator would want to trespass on the liberties of his own or other nations, but such a fanciful notion was wildly unrealistic. It was easily laid down that the dictator must be an honest man; but what if he were not? Pat came the answer that if a dishonest man was chosen, then the country did not deserve good government. Garibaldi commented unhelpfully that one honest man would be more readily found than five hundred.

Of course he had a person like himself in mind, and his own honesty was beyond question. When he also prescribed that the dictator need not be clever because he could find cleverness enough in his ministers, he was again drawing a self-portrait of the ex-Dictator of the Two Sicilies. We find him confessing to a Madrid newspaper that he himself had a full dose of presumption and had committed his share of errors. Evidently he recognized many of his own limitations. But hypocrisy and insincerity were not among them.

As Bandi remarked, Garibaldi had dictatorship in
his blood, just because the type of enterprise he had
happened to command had always needed quick and
unchallenged decisions and blind faith in a leader.
Rationalizing his own experience, he came out with
these general remarks on politics. We need not take
them too seriously. They are not a notable contribution
to political science. But they do throw light on the cast
of Garibaldi's mind and on one of the latent tendencies
inside the Left-wing parties of Italy.

CHAPTER EIGHTEEN

RETROSPECT, PROSPECT, AND FINALE

1881-1882

WITH the acquisition of Rome in 1870 the *risorgimento* seemed to be over. If we leave out of account
the Trentino and Trieste, which Italy secured after
1918, and the farther-flung empire that Crispi and
Mussolini were to insist was the logical development
of national unity, the nation was complete. Garibaldi
had been one of the chief participants in this *risorgimento,* and his retrospective views on it must be of
some interest.

All his life he had pinned his faith on nationalism
as a general solvent of the world's ills. Since Italian
unification had meant a war of liberation against the
oppressive government of Austria, he had assumed
that nationalism went hand in hand with liberation
and so with liberalism. He could not conceive that a
nation which had fought oppression from others could

ever itself be tempted to become an oppressor. Every liberated country would surely have to believe in freedom as a good *per se,* and would have a direct interest in liberating other peoples and giving more freedom to its own. Italy was a case in point. He and most others had assumed that the economic and social backwardness of Italy was due mainly to the ill-will of the old local dynasties, and that the new order would inevitably bring a greatly increased prosperity and an emancipation of the common people from their life of profitless toil and moil.

This was to ask too much, for neither Nature nor human nature was so amenable to reason and man-made laws. Hence Garibaldi's stark disillusionment with the nation as it materialized, though we must remember that his state of health helped to exasperate this pessimism. "It was a different Italy that I had dreamed of all my life," he wrote in 1880, "not this miserable, poverty-stricken, humiliated Italy that we now see, governed by the dregs of the nation."

Looking around him, he just saw apathy everywhere, discord and immorality in every walk of life. Newspapers were corrupt, so were elections, the parliament itself, the magistracy, the administration, the armed services. The army was used by the King not as a protection for the state, but to protect himself against an indignant nation; and parliament was employed to keep Italy rotten and thus easily governable. Garibaldi now openly said in an electoral address that the King had deliberately curtailed the rights of the people and reduced his subjects to lower levels of life than before—so much so that only a dictator with a hand of steel could set things to rights.

Garibaldi concluded that the Italian race must have declined since the great days of ancient Rome, about which he was so fond of reading. Not having any standard of comparison with regard to the worst side of other countries, he painted the seamier side of his own in the blackest colours. The *New York Herald* was almost certainly right, he concluded, in saying that emigrants from Italy were dirtier, less civilized, and less honest than those from anywhere else. The very fact that so many were driven to emigrate was itself a profound condemnation of things as they were.

Italy was a land where the rich flourished and everyone else was miserable. The rich controlled government, and so were able to bias in their own favour both national and local taxes; for they alone had the suffrage and all the secret strings of power. As a result, the great burden of paying for national unification fell on people who reaped the least benefit from it and who in any case could not afford to pay.

At the same time there were higher Court expenses and more civil-list pensions used by the government as a normal means of political bribery. (Perhaps his own pension momentarily escaped this jaundiced scrutiny.) An enormous army was maintained at an expense that made it impossible ever to balance the budget. While every Swiss paid the equivalent of nine lire to be well governed, an Italian paid fifty lire to be governed in a manner that was indescribably bad. A ship in difficulties would go at once on to half-rations— so Garibaldi wrote in one of his notes to parliament —but Italians were becoming more and more wasteful of their few resources the nearer they approached to ruin.

This was too black a picture to be true; yet, with all his ingenuousness and oversimplification, he had the honesty and common sense to comprehend some truths that were hidden from cleverer and better-informed men. It was not simply that unification might not be justified if the masses did not gain from it; the clock might even yet be put back in a terrible counter-revolution if something were not done to convince the peasants that they had more to gain than to lose under the new national regime. As a man of the people, Garibaldi did not breathe that rarefied air of Court and parliament far removed from the odour of sweaty nightcaps. He instinctively saw what few Italian politicians were to see: that the ninety per cent of Italians who worked the land as peasants had somehow to be given a stake in society and so converted into a conservative force; otherwise, they would imperil the very structure of the state.

It was this lack of popular approval, he concluded, which had made Italy lose most of her battles during the process of unification. Lombardy had been won for her by France; Venice and Rome by Prussia. Because the peasants who were the backbone of Italy, hardy and tough fighters, had been enemies rather than friends of the *risorgimento*. Only in Sicily and Calabria had he found much popular enthusiasm, let alone active help from the local inhabitants, for the common people had not looked on the armies of Italy as liberators. Enthusiasm had mostly been reserved for speeches rather than for patriotic action.

He had often seen with his own eyes how the peasants had rejoiced when the Austrians returned to a place after a brief interlude of national "liberation". The unimaginative but efficient and honest Austrian administration had treated them with rough justice, but at least not with crass injustice, whatever the patriotic historians of Italy might say. The new kingdom of Italy, on the other hand, represented not only a harsher tax-collector, but, worse still, it represented the landlords and the bosses. These were the people, the upper and upper-middle classes, who alone had a real practical grievance against Austria, the same people who monopolized government after 1860, and who then manufactured the patriotic mythology that in retrospect softened and justified the movement for national liberation.

The peasants were thus always the first to desert from the Italian army, and would do so the moment a war started going badly. In the south they had been in continual revolution after 1860, and the incessant war against "brigandage" which pinned half the Italian army down in Naples was in reality a war against unemployed and starving labourers who had taken to the hills in protest against the new order. Their answer to bad government was simply a refusal to pay taxes and a refusal to countenance the arbitrary enclosure of common land by their landlords. In the last resort, those who could not afford passage to America might have either to join the *camorra*, that criminal underworld society, or else escape to the hills or the *maquis* and make open war on society. This augured ill for the future of Italy, yet not many people saw this quite so clearly as Garibaldi.

He was far less practised in external politics, and here his views in later life were less consistent and less interesting. During his early years he had been a great conqueror, a pirate and filibuster; and hence the heirs of Garibaldinism—his own children and grandchildren, for instance—sometimes acted as though the whole essence and lesson of his life had been conquest. Crispi and then Mussolini were thus to make a great parade of Garibaldinism, and to claim that in carving out a far-flung African empire they were carrying on the good work of their predecessor.

But this was only half of Garibaldi, for he had always sympathized with people struggling for freedom, in Poland, Crete, Greece, Denmark, Uruguay, or anywhere else. No doubt he assumed that Istria and

Trieste were Italian by right of nationality and could be righteously fought for; yet the defeated Austrians were in every other respect to be treated now as brothers, and he repeatedly asserted that Italy must not intrude on other people's independence. This same right of every nation to be free had been Italy's only justification in her initial struggle against Austria. "A nation does not achieve true greatness at the expense of its neighbours," he wrote to the Press in 1880. If Italy began to be an oppressor, he would even take up arms against his own country.

Likewise, he had little use for colonization, for that would be to put prestige before welfare. Colonization abroad cost money, and would have to be supported by an expensive army and a continual risk of war. The only sensible colonization he could envisage was at home in Italy. Here there were marshes to drain and uncultivated land to clear and irrigate. Put the money into Italy, and then the hundreds of thousands who emigrated abroad would find employment at home and so enrich themselves and their country. How much wiser was this than the later policy of African and Balkan imperialism which brought bankruptcy and humiliating defeat!

Far from being a rampant militarist like the new twentieth-century Garibaldians, their prototype became more and more of a pacifist. As long as the really important questions for Italy were economic, he was sure that the military budget should be heavily cut. A permanent army was a luxury, too heavy a charge for such a poor country. The army also took too many workers away from the fields and put them to unprofitable employment; hence it made Italy dependent on foreign countries for her food, and was therefore one reason for the "deterioration of our race". The government liked to hold the country under an artificial threat of war, and this was done just to inculcate the habit of obedience and keep the opposition quiet; thereby the government was enabled to retain the army for the purpose of curbing internal liberties.

One of Garibaldi's favourite schemes in later years was for international arbitration and a League of Nations. When in prison in 1862 he had sent a memorial to England encouraging her to inaugurate a United States of Europe, at least comprising the "four great Atlantic states". He wrote to Bismarck in 1872 to secure his support for a scheme of arbitration, and warmly commended the example set by America and England. In these Anglo-Saxon countries public opinion was apparently omnipotent and therefore could always fasten on and publicize any genuine scheme of public betterment. He wished he could say as much of Italy.

Garibaldi was very anxious to legitimize his family by Francesca Armosino, the woman who had come to Caprera twenty years before to act as nurse for his other children. He therefore travelled once more to Rome in 1879 to try to secure annulment of his absurd marriage of 1860 with the Marchesina Raimondi. Characteristically, he assumed that the King could and would dissolve this marriage by a dictatorial stroke of the pen, but the King had similar difficulties in his own family and replied that he could not abrogate the law in favour of a single subject, however great. Garibaldi was indignant, and he was equally grieved that his old friend of the Thousand, the prime minister Benedetto Cairoli, would not pass a special nullity decree through parliament.

Crispi then helped him take the case into court, but his suit failed. Discreet pressure seems to have been applied behind the scenes, however, and, despite the protest of certain eminent lawyers, the court of appeal made a second decision finding good reasons for annulment. Garibaldi duly married Francesca just before he died, and both Clelia (b. 1867) and his best-loved, Manlio (b. 1873), were thus enabled to take his name.

Clelia has survived in vigorous health until today, and has contributed many details of the last years before her father's death in 1882. Many of his wife's relatives stayed on and off with them at Caprera. Ricciotti went for a time to America and Australia, Menotti lived with his own family in Rome, Teresita with hers in Genoa. Clelia says that she never saw her father wear anything but a red shirt, and if he ever found that he had more than two shirts, he gave the third away. He smoked a great number of strong Tuscan cigars, and drank much coffee if he sat up writing, sweetening the coffee with honey to save the price of sugar. There was more water than wine at his table, and she remembered him eating raw shrimps, with newspapers doing service as table-cloths. Simplicity and lack of almost any sort of self-indulgence and pomp—these qualities were typical of the man.

He was apparently a great believer in cold water. No sooner was Clelia born than he ducked her in a bath under the terrified eyes of her mother, and later on, as with the other children, he was fond of putting her under a pump. One may wonder if such Spartan treatment, applied to himself, did not encourage his rheumatic ailments. Living on top of the sea, his children were brought up "amphibiously", just as he had been, and he was eager to have his youngest son keep up the family traditions by becoming a sailor.

They were a proud family and stooped to no man. Another scene that Clelia recalled occurred when the mayor of Maddalena came to take away the body of

N

one of Garibaldi's children who had died, as there was no legal cemetery on this lonely island. Her mother threatened to shoot the official, and he hastily retired, leaving them to make their own illegal family burying-ground. Garibaldi also prepared his own funeral pyre, for he had determined to die in the high Roman fashion, in the same pagan and hygienic way he had lived, conforming to no convention or regulation made by other mortals. In death, as in life, he meant to be a law unto himself and captain of his own soul.

Solitude and sickness made him more melancholy as the years went by, but he retained his serene temperament, and Clelia never saw him annoyed or in a temper. He spent his time watching over his estate, or reading and writing, with some gentle carpentry to patch up old furniture, and a little tailoring with scissors and needle to keep himself in clothes. Sometimes, especially when Teresita was there to play the piano, his baritone voice was heard in certain favourite arias from Verdi and Donizetti.

He was too crippled now to do much active work on the farm. Guerzoni says that about a third of the island had been rendered fruitful, but this is probably an exaggeration. Until 1870 he had gone out regularly every morning, always in red shirt and wide-brimmed hat, with scissors and knives at his belt, to prune and graft his trees. There were about ten acres of cereals at the most, but neither these nor his so-called vineyards were ever worth the money spent on them, so low was the yield. There were some machines from England, and as many as a hundred and fifty head of cattle and four hundred sheep, and a great number of sheds, stables, dovecotes and beehives.

Guerzoni also tells us of his library. He read a little of everything, without being in any sense a great reader, and probably he wrote more than he read. His mind had a natural bent towards physical science, and he possessed a number of treatises on mathematics and agriculture. He was particularly fond of Greek and Roman history. Voltaire was also a favourite author. But chiefly he liked poetry, especially patriotic poetry, and an open copy of Foscolo was by his deathbed.

Garibaldi was never a rich man. His savings, his brother's legacy, his several government pensions, and the many gifts he received from all over the world—all went down into the bottomless pit of Caprera as he tried to make a granite outcrop into a productive farm. For twenty years he spent lavishly, and with little return except in contentment and self-sufficiency. At one time there was much talk of his poverty and he had to protest publicly against this, explaining that he always adjusted himself to whatever he possessed, and liked doing so. His children did not make a very good living—especially Ricciotti, who indulged unwisely in heavy speculation on building construction in Rome. They sometimes tended to look to him for support, and some of the family were not above exploiting and publicizing his penury.

When the government offered him a pension (against an opposition vote of only twenty-five) he had at first proudly refused, saying that he would not be corrupted by the government at the price of further impoverishing the country, and that he would have been ashamed to look on really poor people ever again. When finally he took a substantial payment from Depretis, he did so under considerable pressure, for the government feared that his creditors might make him bankrupt and so show up the country as ungrateful.

Garibaldi's last few years were labour and sorrow to him and to his friends. Feet and hands were cruelly twisted with arthritis, and he could move only in a wheeled chair. Once he insisted on travelling to Milan, but when he appeared in public it was motionless and prostrate on a bed, and a minister in parliament described the scene and his reception as if it had been the catafalque of a miracle-working saint. The ashen colour and white beard of this revenant came as a great shock to the citizens lining the streets, for whom he was already a dauntless hero of distant legend.

The advice of his doctors was to leave Caprera for a warmer climate, but he refused: the sea and the solitude were too dear to him. Only after being badly shaken in a fall did he agree to go to Naples for his health, and then his bed had to be lifted up bodily by crane. There he lived for a time in the Villa Maclean at Posillipo, and crowds came out by sea and land to see him and pay their respects.

After this he obstinately resolved on visiting Sicily for the sexcentenary of that event known as the "Sicilian Vespers", the day in 1282 when Sicilians had risen against their French overlords in a fierce day of slaughter. He chose this anniversary on purpose. It would be a fine occasion for reawakening the national spirit, which he had reason to fear was especially weak in this southernmost tip of Italy.

The crowds in Palermo were deathly silent as the pallid, mute, stiff figure was borne through the streets. Already he had entered the folk consciousness of Sicilians as one more of the countless conquerors who had enriched and impoverished their island. In puppet shows and in coloured rustic woodcarvings he was already becoming confused with Saladin and Richard Cœur de Lion and paragons of the remote past. Legends were already current in the south that this was not the same Garibaldi who had come in 1860. People were murmuring as they watched him that, with his magic shirt, the real Garibaldi could never suffer mortality.

Shortly afterwards, back in Caprera, he died quietly on June 2, 1882, at the age of seventy-four years and eleven months. A young naval doctor from a nearby ship had been called in to treat the bronchial catarrh that made breathing so difficult, but nothing could be done. Several of the little birds that he used to feed came and perched on the window ledge, and almost his last remark was that they might be the spirits of two of his dead children; he enjoined that they be cared for after his death.

The dead man had often expressed the wish to be cremated on a high wooden pyre like one of Homer's heroes. In his will he bade his wife not to tell the authorities of his dying until this had been done. She should prepare aromatic wood of aloes and myrtle from Caprera. His body should be decked in a red shirt and burned defiantly under the open sky. Then the ashes should be placed in a crystal bottle and interred beneath his favourite juniper tree. A later appendix to the will added that she would need plenty of wood.

But the dignitaries of Rome, whom he had always execrated alive, would not be done out of a good funeral, and were revenged on him dead. As an added touch of irony, it was argued that burning would offend people's religious sensibilities. The authorities were in time to overrule his wife, and were supported in this by his children. He was incongruously buried in the presence of dukes, ministers, and deputies, while survivors of the Thousand carried the bier. The world had the last word against him.

His own last word was a Political Testament. To his children and friends he bequeathed his love for liberty and truth. He explicitly repudiated the last ministry of what he called that atrocious foe of humankind, the Catholic priesthood. Once more he condemned the Mazzinians as enemies of Italy and little better than the priests. And again he recommended that his countrymen select the most honest man in Italy and make him a temporary dictator. Only when Italians were more educated to liberty, and their country was less threatened from outside, should dictatorial rule give way to a regular republican government. Here in brief was a neat abstract of the lessons learned by a simple-minded but strong-hearted soldier during a lifetime of devotion to an ideal.

INDEX

OTHER BOOKS

DUMAS, ALEXANDRE: *On Board the "Emma"; Adventures with Garibaldi's "Thousand" in Sicily.* Translated by R. S. Garnett. London: Ernest Benn; 1929 and 1931.

GARIBALDI, GIUSEPPE: *Autobiography,* edited by A. Werner. Three volumes, of which the third volume is a supplement by Jessie White Mario. London: W. Smith & Innes; 1889.

——: *Edizione Nazionale degli Scritti di.* Six volumes. Bologna; 1932-7.

GUERZONI, GIUSEPPE: *Garibaldi.* Two volumes. Firenze: G. Barbera; 1882.

MACK SMITH, D.: *Cavour and Garibaldi, 1860.* Cambridge: Cambridge University Press; 1954.

MARIO, JESSIE WHITE: *The Birth of Modern Italy,* posthumous papers. T. Fisher Unwin; 1909.

SACERDOTE, GUSTAVO: *La Vita di Giuseppe Garibaldi.* Milano; 1933.

SCHWARTZ, MARIE ESPÉRANCE VON: *Garibaldi: Recollections of his Public and Private Life.* London: Trübner & Co.; 1887.

TREVELYAN, GEORGE MACAULAY: *Garibaldi and the Making of Italy.* London: Longmans, Green & Co.; 1911.

——: *Garibaldi and the Thousand.* London: Longmans, Green & Co.; 1909.

——: *Garibaldi's Defence of the Roman Republic.* London: Longmans, Green & Co.; 1907.

VECCHI, AUGUSTO: *Garibaldi at Caprera,* with a preface by Mrs. Gaskell. London: Macmillan; 1862.

DENIS MACK SMITH

was born in London and educated at Cambridge University, where he has been, since 1947, a Fellow and Tutor of Peterhouse and Lecturer at the University. One of the outstanding younger British historians, he established his reputation as an authority on nineteenth-century Italy with his Cavour and Garibaldi: 1860. *He is also the author of the forthcoming* A History of Italy: 1860-1957.